D1830469

INDIA AND THE EMPIRE

INDIA AND THE EMPIRE

A LECTURE AND VARIOUS PAPERS ON INDIAN GRIEVANCES

ANNIE BESANT

GYAN

Published by

Gyan Publishing House
5, Ansari Road
Daryaganj, New Delhi-110002
Phone: 011-47034999, 9811692060
E-mail: books@gyanbooks.com

Distribution Network
gyanbooks.com
India, USA, Canada, UK, Australia, France

© Publisher

All rights reserved. No part of this work may be reproduced, stored, adapted, or transmitted in any form or by any means, electronic, mechanical, photocopying, micro-filming, recording or otherwise, or translated in any language, without the prior written permission of the copyright owner and the publisher.

ISBN: 978-81-212-8836-1 (PB)
First Published, 1914

2nd Impression 2023

Printed at: Gyan Press, Delhi.

The book is sold subject to the condition that it shall not, by way of trade or otherwise, be lent, resold, hired out, or otherwise circulated without the prior publisher's written consent.

INDIA AND THE EMPIRE
Author: Annie Besant

INDIA AND THE EMPIRE

A LECTURE AND VARIOUS PAPERS ON INDIAN GRIEVANCES

BY

ANNIE BESANT

LONDON
THEOSOPHICAL PUBLISHING SOCIETY
161 NEW BOND STREET, W.
1914

PREFACE

The ignorance of the English public as to things relating to India, and the indifference of the House of Commons—as shown by the empty benches when Indian questions are before it—are grave dangers to the Empire. India is asking for self-government, such as is enjoyed by the Colonies, and she earnestly desires to have her place within the circle of the Empire, under the ægis of the Crown. Western education has inspired Western ideals of representation and self-government, and responsible Englishmen have declared that England desired to give to India the liberties enjoyed by her own people, so soon as India was ready to possess and utilise them. India has grown to love these ideals and to aspire after self-control; she does not seek to break her link with England, but she desires so to transform it that it may be a tie honourable to both and prized by both. She cannot remain the only nation in the Empire which is held in dependence, while she sees younger and less civilised peoples enjoying national autonomy.

I feel convinced that if the British public understood the reasonableness and the urgency of India's plea for justice, her demand would be heard and granted. Britain is indifferent because ignorant. The following papers have appeared during the last few weeks, and some interest, at least, has been aroused. They are now published separately, in the hope of reaching fresh readers, and of arousing further interest.

A brief explanation as to *The Times* correspondence is needed. My original letter appeared on May 29, 1914, and was followed on May 30 by the leader, reprinted here by the courteous permission of the Editor. There was no need to reply to this, as it evaded the main points, and its suggestion of my ignorance of well-known Indian conditions was merely foolish. But on June 3, Miss Cornelia Sorabji, a Parsi by birth and a Christian by belief, rushed into the field, and made various misstatements as to ancient Indian ideals, calculated to mislead the public. *The Times* farther printed a contradiction from the Institution of Civil Engineers of one of my statements. I waited to see if any other comments would be made, and, as none appeared, I sent a reply on June 14. I received a note that the Editor hoped to print it; I waited a week, and then wrote asking that my letter might be returned, as I had kept no copy, not thinking it possible that a paper of the standing of *The Times* would not print a reply to misstatements it had inserted. Again I had note of the Editor's continuing hope, and a proof of the letter. Another week is drawing to its close, and I am leaving to-night for India, so I print here my reply to Miss Sorabji: it may have appeared before this booklet sees the light. Lālā Lajpat Rai, a Hindu, wrote exposing Miss Sorabji's ignorance of Hinduism, but his letter was refused insertion. Miss Sorabji writes as though Indian traditions and ideals were dear to her, but she does not share them, having been born a Parsi and having embraced Christianity; her arguments should only be taken at their face value, not as having the weight belonging to a member of the faith she misrepresents. Her ignorance of Hinduism is quite excusable under the circumstances, and is indeed natural. But the public would imagine from her letter that she was a Hindu.

The papers are printed in the order of their publication, except that *The Times* correspondence is all printed consecutively.

I am very grateful to the Editors of *The Christian Commonwealth*, *The Nation*, *The Daily Chronicle*, and *The Daily News* for their friendly help in laying facts before the public. My gratitude is also due to the Editor of *The Times* for the insertion of my first letter. I wish he had been fair enough to print my reply before all public interest had died out; and "pressure on space" is hardly a satisfactory reason for a fortnight's delay, where so much that appears is of no immediate importance, and is of limited interest. The exigencies of party politics now outweigh the old journalistic fairness, and facts which do not suit the favourite party are too often suppressed. Our daily newspapers neither lead nor express public opinion, nor care much for public interest. They rather try to suppress all that is against the party which they represent, and to exaggerate all that they think will help it. It seems a pity.

LONDON,
June 26th, 1914.

CONTENTS

	PAGE
A Plea for India	11
India and Australia	25
India and the Empire	30
The Problem of India	40
The Voice of the East	47
Mrs Besant and India	55
Mrs Besant and India	57
Present Day Problems	62
Colour Bar in the Dominions	71
East and West	80
Lajpat Rai and British Citizenship	88
The Indian Problem	94
India, a Buttress or a Peril?	100
India's Plea for Justice	103

INDIA AND THE EMPIRE

A PLEA FOR INDIA

THE INDIAN NATIONAL CONGRESS DEPUTATION

(*The Christian Commonwealth*, May 13, 1914)

In the present crash and turmoil of home politics the visit of the Indian National Congress Deputation to England runs a chance of being overlooked; yet the welfare and content of India is a matter of no less importance to the Empire than the pacification of the militant unrest in Ireland, and distance blinds the self-centred home population to the growing alienation from Great Britain of her huge "dependency." The British public has never yet set itself to face the Indian problem; it thinks vaguely of India as a half-civilised country, benevolently ruled for its own good by "the best Civil

Service in the world," and when it hears of unrest and discontent it piously wonders at the ingratitude returned for the blessings bestowed upon it. It knows nothing of the great and ancient civilisation which existed ere Athens rose and Rome was founded; it knows not that Greek philosophers sought wisdom from India, and that the literature which still dominates Europe drew largely from Indian thought; it knows not that the trade and commerce of India spread westwards to Asia Minor and to Egypt, that her manufactures were eagerly sought for by Roman patricians, that in the Middle Ages Venice and Holland grew wealthy by the import of her products, that European travellers in the days of the Stuarts wrote in amazement of her art and of the wealth and luxury abounding on every side, and that even in the middle of the eighteenth century Phillimore wrote that "the droppings of her soil fed distant regions." The better educated have a vague idea of the more modern part of her literature, of the dramas of Kalidasa, of the poems of Tulsidas and Kabir, of the philosophical writings of

Shankaracharya, Ramanuja, and Madhoa, of the inspiring ethics of Nanak and Tukaram; but even they do not realise that Indian literature does not belong only to really ancient times, but rolls down in an unbroken stream to the eighteenth century, and is of unparalleled beauty and richness. What does the English democracy know of the great modern Indian kingdoms, of the strength and magnificence of the Mughal Empire, the splendid achievements of the Maratha power? Arrogant Englishmen speak of the want of initiative and of power of organisation in Indians, forgetting all their modern triumphs as well as their ancient glory, and calmly ignoring the record even of the last fifty years, with the great prime ministers of Indian States—States which, in many respects, are advancing more rapidly than British India. People speak of the Pax Britannica, but forget that when the East India Company came to India it came because it was attracted by the extraordinary wealth and prosperity of the country, and that the existence of such wealth proved that a stable and secure civilisation existed, despite the wars of rival chiefs. Banks, credit, wealthy merchants spoke eloquently of the state of civilisation then existing, and of the initiative and power of organisation of the Indians who lived under it. The unrestrained export of her foodstuffs, due to the railways, caused far more numerous and more widely spread famines than did the occasional destruction of crops by war in a restricted locality. The prevalence of malaria, largely due to the swamps created by embankments, which prevent the old free course of water into the rivers, and the ravages of plague, which is now practically established all over India—these things are a heavy offset to the Pax Britannica. And the broad fact remains that India *was* rich and *is* poor.

It is clear, however, that with the growth of the West the old civilisations of the East could not have remained unmodified, and India, like other nations, would, in any case, have been obliged to pass into a new condition of things. Many of us believe that, in the wider issues, the coming of British rule into India will prove ultimately to be for the good of both nations and of the world at large. English education forced the ablest of the Indian people to imbibe the modern spirit, and a new love of liberty began to stir in their hearts and to inspire their minds. They eagerly drank the milk of the new spirit at England's breast, and there was a moment when, had England grasped the opportunity, the gratitude of India would have enshrined her in India's heart. India looked to England as the mother of free institutions, and, new to these Western methods, would have gladly learned them at her hands. The National Congress was founded, India's first effort to imitate the representative system, and to lay before the Ruling Power, by the voice of her representatives, her needs, her troubles, and her hopes. It is idle to say that the Congress does not represent India; every such body represents first a section of the more advanced of the nation as the burgesses of Edward I. were the first representatives of the Commonalty of England; popular institutions must grow; they cannot spring full-armed as Minerva from the head of Jove. The National Congress is India articulate and self-conscious, and the little regard paid to it in England, the lack of sympathy, nay, the utter blindness shown to the extraordinary initiative and power of organisation proved during the twenty-eight years of the life of this National Parliament—the only strength of which lies in the voluntary obedience and the self-disciplined co-operation of the educated class—all this has embittered the India that erst believed, but now disbelieves, in England's love of liberty. How can she believe in it in face of the Arms Act, the Press Act, the house searchings, the espionage, the autocracy, the frustration of her dearest hopes, the treatment of her noblest as inferiors, the utter disregard of the promises made in 1858? When England sees outrages in any other country she primly says that the Government ought to redress the grievances which cause them, and not crush out the symptoms and punish free expression, and she opens her arms to the political refugees. When she meets them in her own dominions she forgets her advice to others, falls back on the very methods she condemns, sees sedition in every appeal to right wrongs, and she, who sheltered and protected Stepniak, a leader of the Terror and an advocate of political assassination, on the ground that his crimes were political, refuses to recognise any difference between political and ordinary crime in her own dominions. She says, as Russia said, that "murder is murder." I think she is right in this, and that those who use bombs cannot logically object to hanging; but is it consistent to give sanctuary to foreign murderers and to hang Indian boys for similar crimes? However this may be, India wants no murderers, and her educated classes detest crime, political or other. The anarchical movement is alien, not native, and is inspired and directed from abroad. The National Congress has steadfastly worked along constitutional lines; the attempt by the party of violence to capture it at Surat met with ignominious failure; it stands as the representative of orderly and constitutional progress, and asks only that India shall be recognised as a nation, shall be given self-government, and shall form an integral part of the Empire, composed of self-governing communities. She asks no more than this; *she will be satisfied with nothing less.* It is treason to the Empire to conceal this fact, and to cry "Peace, peace," when there is no peace. India is willing that the change from foreign autocracy to self-government shall come gradually, but it must come steadily; the aim must be recognised and the progress towards it must be perceptible.

The Deputation has come to lay before English statesmen certain definite matters, and the requests it brings are—like all the Congress proposals—eminently reasonable and moderate.

On July 31, 1913, Lord Crewe announced the reconstruction of the India Council, and invited criticism and suggestions. India sends them. She wants no India Council at all, but, recognising that England will not give up the anachronism, she proffers a proposal for its improvement, basing her requests on the statements made by Mr Disraeli and Lord Stanley in the Commons, and Lord Derby in the Lords, when the India Bill was before Parliament in 1858. The then Government stated, through Lord

Stanley, "We are willing to introduce the elective principle," but they found themselves estopped by two difficulties, the disturbed state of the country after the Sepoy insurrection, and the impossibility of finding "a fitting and satisfactory constituency." Both these difficulties have disappeared; there is no disturbance in India of a serious nature, the whole country is enthusiastically loyal to the Crown, and the constituency is provided by the Minto-Morley reforms.

The new difficulty is that while educated India has been moving steadily forward in the love of liberty and the use of representative institutions, England has been as steadily retrogressing from all her old traditions, and that which Tories were anxious to give in 1858 is denied by Radicals in 1914. The practice of autocracy has corrupted the mother of free institutions, and the Deputation comes to ask England to close the widening gulf by returning to the position of 1858, where India has stood, waiting patiently, for six-and-fifty years. The Deputation proposes that one-third of the council shall be elected by non-official India, and that, of the remaining two-thirds, half shall be nominated from men of capacity and merit, unconnected with Indian administration, and the second half nominated from Anglo-Indian officials, who have served for not less than ten years and have not been out of India for more than two. Surely no proposal could be more moderate; two-thirds of the council are to be nominated, so that the elected members are in a continual minority. But Congress feels that where India's case is good, the non-official third of men of light and leading will be with her. She asks also that the council may be advisory, not legislative, so that the responsibility of the Secretary of State to Parliament shall be complete. Will a so-called Liberal Government dare to refuse this modest prayer?

The Deputation asks also for the long-discussed separation of executive and judicial functions, so that suitors, lawyers, and witnesses may not have to travel after the collector, intent on revenue business, at heavy cost of time and money, and often find themselves before a tired magistrate, who writes on other business while counsel are pleading, and disposes of cases by intuition rather than by evidence. If "British justice" in country districts is no longer to be sneered at, this reform must be granted.

Two other matters of vital moment are to be pressed—the repeal of the Press Act, or, if that be refused, the introduction into the Act of an amendment making real the illusory protection of the High Courts—*i.e.* carrying out the pledge given by the Government, on the faith of which Indian Councillors voted for the Bill. The friction caused by the foolish action of ill-advised magistrates is dangerous, and is growing worse and worse; a common peril is welding Hindus and Mahomedans together—and for this we may be thankful; but the resistance engendered is angry, bitter, and dangerous, and over this lovers of the Empire cannot rejoice. Moreover, the Act is very unfairly administered. Papers conducted by Englishmen are allowed to insult Indians to any extent, and the magistracy, Nelson-like, turns on them only its blind eye. But it is Argus-eyed towards Indian papers, and the

Mahomedan public is seething with indignation over the late treatment of its journals.

The second question is the position of Indians outside India. This cannot be evaded, for on the answer to it the safety of the Empire depends. South Africa—thanks to Lord Hardinge and to the agitation carried on by Indians on behalf of their countrymen—is probably settled for the moment. It has done its work. It has welded together all classes and the two sexes in public patriotic agitation. Indian women have held meetings, made speeches, collected funds—an unexampled uprising of Indian womanhood of the profoundest significance and moment for the future. All distinctions of caste have equally been flung aside, and all united in a common protest. Lord Hardinge, with a statesman's insight, saw the approaching danger, and, like Richard II., put himself at the head of the surging crowds ere they broke into tumult. The lesson of what India united can do will never be forgotten, and will be utilised in the future. The question remains: Will Great Britain remain idle while the Colonies wreck the Empire, and while the United States justify the exclusion of Indians by their example? What have Indians done that they alone, of all the nations of the world, should be pent within their own land, into which every foreigner may tramp unchecked? All may have their will of India, may swarm over her soil, exploit her resources, and insult her people with the assertion of their fancied superiority. Indians alone are to find every door shut in their faces abroad, while the highest posts in their own land are also closed against them. Cannot England see the intolerable position into which she is allowing the whole Indian nation to be forced? There are three hundred millions of people in India; education is spreading; communications are open; the people read and understand what is passing all over the world. They are still patient and forbearing, but they are growing more bitter and estranged every month. The situation is becoming maddening, and it cannot last. A whole nation cannot be held for ever in thrall and confined within its own borders, forbidden expansion without while denied freedom within. India sends to England a deputation of worthy, sober-judging, reliable, quiet men. These are no wild extremists, no mad theorists; they are patriots; lovers of liberty, loyal subjects of the Crown, would-be citizens of the Empire. They ask for the primary rights of educated human beings, freedom to take part in the government of their own country, freedom to travel, as others travel, within the Empire, freedom to earn their bread by the labour of their own brains and their own hands. They plead for a nation of three hundred millions, which would love England and defend her Empire, if fairly treated. Will England treat their plea with denial or contempt?

ANNIE BESANT.

INDIA AND AUSTRALIA

AN INTERVIEW WITH MRS ANNIE BESANT

BY RHODE KNIGHT

(*The British-Australasian*, May 28, 1914)

ALTHOUGH nearly twenty years have elapsed since Mrs Annie Besant paid her first memorable visit to Sydney and Melbourne, the deep impression she then made still remains on the minds of those who were privileged to meet her. Her sweet womanliness and fascinating charm of manner, not less than the breadth of her intellect, the loftiness of her spirit, and her thrilling eloquence, cast a spell upon all with whom she came in contact. One had not necessarily to share all her ideals or to see eye to eye in regard to all the great problems of life in order to experience the uplifting power of her influence and teaching. Mystery environs us, and mysticism has ever appealed to the human mind; Mrs Besant, as the high priestess of Theosophy, appeared to many as a torch-bearer, guiding them along untrodden or little-known paths. And in the more practical affairs of life her influence and teaching were perhaps even more potent.

Her mission to Australia in 1895 has had an abiding effect—an effect which became more marked after her visit in 1908. The work of the Society of which she is the head is growing.

"It is spreading," she said to me; "not very rapidly, but, I think, in a very solid way. We are not as strong in the Oversea Dominions as we are in the Mother Country, in America, and in India. In Australia we have only 22 lodges and a little over 1200 active members. But they *are* active. In New Zealand we have 22 lodges and 820 members. Those are the figures for last year. The work grows steadily there, and a great deal is being done by sending books to all the public libraries and to the schools.

"One phase of our work is particularly interesting and encouraging. I refer to a children's society, called The Golden Chain, which has a membership of between nine and ten thousand in Australia alone. The rules are very simple. The children are expected to make a little promise every morning that they will be kind to all living creatures, that they will try to speak only good and gentle words, and think good and gentle thoughts. The Society has been taken up a good deal in the schools, and the membership, I am glad to say, is growing very, very quickly.

"I am hoping to revisit Australia—not this year, but the year after next," said Mrs Besant in reply to my inquiry. "Next year I must go to America to attend the Philosophical Congress at 'Frisco."

In discussing public opinion in India—that is, the opinion of the educated Indians themselves—in regard to Australia's policy of excluding all coloured races, even though they may be subjects of the British Crown and citizens of the Empire, Mrs Besant observed:—

"They express themselves very strongly

in regard to Australia's attitude. They wish, indeed, to have Australians excluded from India unless Indians are admitted to Australia. They wish, too, to impose prohibitory duties upon Australian products. People here do not realise how radically India has changed, even within the last ten or fifteen years. Education is spreading; the people know what is passing in the world; there is a growing national feeling; and when they find all the Colonies excluding them they are fired by a desire to pass retaliatory laws.

"I believe in the Empire," exclaimed Mrs Besant, her face lighting with enthusiasm, "and it is the best kindness to the Empire to speak out and let people know the truth. Some people think that by voicing it the danger is increased. I don't; I think it is diminished. The Indians are a patient and forbearing race, but their patience and forbearance are being taxed beyond endurance. Three hundred millions of people cannot be held for ever in thrall, confined within their own gates, forbidden expansion without and denied freedom within. A rude and sudden awakening must come if Great Britain and the Empire persist in ignoring India's just claims for freedom and equality. They are loyal at present, but existing conditions are straining their loyalty to breaking point."

INDIA AND THE EMPIRE

PROBLEMS FOR STATESMEN

MRS BESANT'S VIEW OF NATIVE GRIEVANCES

(*The Times*, Friday, May 29, 1914)

To the Editor of *The Times*.

SIR,—Outside the domestic problems of Ulster and the women's war, Great Britain is faced with two problems in the East which will tax to the utmost her political sagacity, and it is not too much to say that her success or failure in building a world-Empire will depend on the fashion of their solution.

The first is that of Indian emigration, and the right of Indians to travel freely throughout the Empire and to settle in it where they will. This chiefly affects the labouring classes of the vast Indian population, seeking an outlet for subsistence abroad, since many of the home industries have ceased to be life-supporting; to some extent their difficulties in gaining a livelihood in India may be diminished by the demand for labour in tea, coffee, and other plantations, where wages tend to rise in consequence of the scarcity of coolies, and by the improvement of village life by the spread of co-operation and the revival of weaving and other handicrafts. These remedial tendencies are, however, inevitably slow in their action, and the area over which they must spread for effective usefulness is so huge that, while they may slightly lessen they cannot obviate the necessity for emigration in search of livelihood. The educated class is touched by the question of the emigration of the labouring population mainly through sentiment—the feelings of kinship with those immediately affected, of indignation against unfair treatment meted out to fellow-countrymen, of race-pride smarting under the imputation of inferiority. The late agitation in India over the South African troubles—that had risen to danger-point when Lord Hardinge's statesman-like sympathy saved the situation by associating the Government with the popular feeling—joined all classes together for the first time in a national protest, and made India feel her strength as a united people; its practical success in gaining a large measure of relief is hailed as a sign that Indian public opinion is no longer voiceless and impotent, and that Indian feeling can be effectively aroused in defence of Indian interests. To the educated class this question of emigration is only part of the larger problem—the position of Indians in the Empire as inferiors or as equals; and it is this second question which is greatly the more important, although the emigration matter may seem to be more immediately pressing.

The Ideal of Liberty

Since the famous educational minute of Lord Macaulay, England has steadily held up before the eyes of the youths receiving English education in Government schools and colleges the ideals of English liberty, English constitutional government, English systems of local and national self-rule; she has aroused Indian admiration for her ordered freedom, for her warm sympathy with autocratically governed nations when they strove to win their liberty, for her shelter of political refugees, and her refusal to surrender to infuriated Governments those who had taken sanctuary on her soil after the commission of political crimes. Several generations of Indians have grown up in the belief that England loved liberty, that when she saw political unrest she advised rulers to seek its causes and to remove them, that repression of the voicing of complaints was folly, as it merely increased discontent by driving it under the surface, and, further, that the repressive policy only deprived the Government of the advantage of knowing what its subjects were thinking, and thus of remedying grievances which might cause serious danger when concealed.

The events of the last few years have inflicted a rude shock on these beliefs; Indians who have been taught the value of liberty, that "taxation without representation is robbery," that "Government rests on the will of the people," find that what England treasures for herself she refuses to them. And they find, with still greater pain, that England, face to face with political crimes, adopts all the methods she has hitherto blamed in others—repression of free speech, prohibition of public meetings, securities from the Press forfeited by the arbitrary will of the Executive, house-searchings by the police, deportation without trial, detention in prison without trial, proclamation of districts entailing the necessity of obtaining permission for any public meeting, police espionage, etc., Russian methods used by free England, and the forfeiture of the freedom of all law-abiding people because a few desperadoes have committed crimes. No one who does not live as a friend among Indians can know the deep resentment felt by them against such methods employed by a country they loved and admired. The suspicion of their loyalty shown by Government has bred suspicion in them, and there is a widening gulf between the officials and the educated class.

The growing sense of self-respect, of

patriotism, and of public spirit, fostered by English education and by contact with Englishmen, will no longer accept benevolent patronage with gratitude; Indians demand to be treated as equals, and not as a "subject race"; they refuse to regard colour as a disqualification for any office in a coloured nation, and demand that Queen Victoria's proclamation of 1858—India's Magna Charta, as they fondly call it—shall no longer remain a dead letter. The best men are standing out of Government service because they will not tolerate supersession by Englishmen inferior to themselves, merely on the ground of colour, and because they will not subject themselves to arrogance and discourtesy. They say frankly that the best men no longer come out to India, whether as judges, civilians, or professors, and that fifth-rate Englishmen should not be preferred to first-rate Indians. They claim at least equality in Government service, and some say that where qualifications are equal the Indian should be preferred in his own country to the foreigner. Government service will be increasingly manned by an inferior class of Indians unless conditions are altered and colour ceases to be regarded as a mark of inferiority.

I leave aside here questions of social difficulties: the exclusion of Indians from clubs, the insults often offered to them if they travel first-class on railways, the refusal to admit them to railway bedrooms at night, the readiness to strike men of the lower classes and even sometimes of the higher, the light punishments inflicted where a blow or a kick causes death, the keeping of Indian gentlemen waiting in verandahs sometimes for hours when they visit officials—a whole long list of social affronts which cause unending bitterness. The Indians say that social equality will only come with political equality, and I believe they are right.

Political Demands

Their political demands are easily formulated. The National Congress and the Muslim League both demand self-government—self-government within the Empire. They demand that the representation granted by the Minto-Morley reforms shall be made effective, by not outnumbering the representatives on the Supreme and Provincial Legislatures with official members; the representatives are in a perpetual minority, and can only criticise, they cannot legislate. Gradually, all members of such bodies should be elected, and the Government should be responsible to the Legislature.

The Press Act must be abolished, and Press criticism must not be regarded as sedition. The sweeping clauses of the Act can catch legitimate criticism within the net of sedition, and every Indian editor lives under the sword of Damocles. The promise of protection by the revision of the High Court has proved to be a delusion, and amendment at least should be granted if abolition be refused.

Indian candidates for the Services should be placed on an equality with English ones by the establishment of simultaneous examinations; at present the Imperial Services, which give higher social position and higher pay—the Civil Service, the Medical, the Educational, the Bar, the Engineering—can only be entered by residence in England.

When the youths come over to England they find difficulties placed in their way; the Universities of Oxford and Cambridge restrict admission, the medical colleges are doing the same, the Bar has raised the conditions of admission, the Institute of Engineers demands higher qualifications from the Indian than from the English students.

The separation of the executive and judicial functions of the magistrates is needed for the fair administration of justice; counsel, witnesses, litigants have to follow an inconsiderate magistrate who fixes a place twenty miles away for a hearing, to suit his convenience for other work. The unfairness is admitted, but no remedy is found.

Representation on the India Council is asked for, and this will probably be granted, though to a lesser degree than is asked.

Now that there is talk of federating the Empire, this question of India becomes pressing. Great Britain, Ireland, the Colonies are spoken of as federated countries; India is always left out. If she is shut out of the Empire, as a self-governing country, will she be to blame if she refuses to remain in it as a dependency? If her sons are shut out of the Colonies, will she be to blame if she shuts out all colonials? If the white man lords it over the Asiatic outside Asia, shall not the Asiatic be at least his own master within Asia? The educated Indian is a highly cultured, courteous, noble-hearted, patriotic gentleman; is he always to be shut out from the best in his own country? Is he never to be free among free men? Is he never to be estimated by his character, his brain, and his heart, but always by the colour of his skin? There is no finer class in the Empire than that composed of the educated Indians. They offer an intelligent loyalty, the loyalty of citizens and of free men. Ill will it be for the Empire if it rejects their love and disregards their loyalty. For India is awakened into national self-consciousness, and her tie with Great Britain can only be preserved by her freedom. Free, she will be the buttress of the Empire; subject, she will be a perpetual menace to its stability.—I am, etc.,

ANNIE BESANT.

LONDON, *May 28.*

THE PROBLEM OF INDIA

(*The Times*, May 30, 1914)

THE letter from Mrs Besant which we published yesterday draws attention in a very fair-minded way to certain spacious problems affecting the future of British rule in India, but it is materially weakened by an imperfect understanding of Indian conditions. Mrs Besant, for example, has clearly paid very little attention to the question of Indian emigration. She assumes, as so many people assume, that India is already over-populated, and that such incidents as the shipload of Indians now clamouring for admission to British Columbia are due to the fact that India is overcrowded. This is not the case, and the fact has a very close connection with the Canadian problem now attracting worldwide attention. The truth is that no region in Asia has at present more population than it can comfortably support, with the possible exception of Japan. Even China could easily maintain far more than her present myriads. Persia is half empty, and the fertile but desolate lands of Mesopotamia cry aloud for efficient labour. To no country are these statements more applicable than to India. It is perfectly true that in Bengal, and perhaps in certain small areas of the Punjab, the average population per square mile is excessive. The correct remedy lies not in emigration, but in measures for spreading the people in more equal proportion over the cultivable land, and still more in attracting them to the manufacturing industries now growing up in India. We recommend Mrs Besant to consult the millowners of Cawnpore, or the employers of labour in Bombay. They will tell her that, despite India's millions, and despite the comparatively high wages they offer, they find the greatest difficulty in manning their mills and factories with efficient labour. The real explanation of the episodes now attracting so much attention on the Pacific coast of Canada is that certain sections of the Indian population have become infected with the "get-rich-quick" craze which is working so much harm throughout both North and South America. An enterprising and lucky peasant from the Punjab makes a few thousand dollars in British Columbia. Instantly he writes to all his friends and relations to come and do likewise. We can conceive no land and no climate where the people of the Punjab are less likely to become useful colonists, descending from generation to generation, than British Columbia. No desire for the vindication of the rights of Indians as subjects of the Empire, but rather that desperate acquisitiveness which is always at the bottom of the motives of the Sikh, is the true explanation of the appearance of the steamer *Komagata Maru* at Vancouver.

In other respects, Mrs Besant's letter fails to face examination. Even her "facts" will not bear the test of scrutiny. It is not true, as she suggests, that the Provincial Legislatures in India contain a majority of official representatives. The unofficial members preponderate, and even in the Imperial Legislative Council the late Lord Minto was willing to relinquish the official majority until he was overruled—in our opinion correctly—by Lord Morley. When Mrs Besant complains that some Indian litigants have to journey twenty miles to get their cases heard she makes the cause she pleads ridiculous. Rural litigants will always have to make journeys, unless the house of every man is converted into a Court of Appeal. We are convinced, after careful inquiry, that Indians suffer no definite disabilities in this respect which are not shared by their fellow-subjects in England, and we think it would be kinder to India to make litigation more difficult instead of easier. We are, further, unable to associate ourselves with Mrs Besant's criticism of the Press Acts in India. No one who has intimate knowledge of the Indian vernacular Press can doubt that in India the privileges enjoyed by conductors of newspapers have been in some instances very greatly abused in the last decade. To assess the extent of the damage which has been wrought it is necessary to sit, not in a college at Benares, but with the village schoolmaster beneath the banyan tree which furnishes a common resting-place at eventide. There is no restriction inflicted nowadays upon the Indian Press which would not sit lightly and imperceptibly upon any editor in England. The English editor knows the bounds beyond which he should not transgress; the Indian editor has no tradition of restraint.

We have not the slightest desire to evade the larger issues raised by Mrs Besant, whose long and sympathetic association with the people of India is now recognised by them and by us. Although she does not explicitly say so, her letter touches upon the whole immense question of the grounds for the presence of the British in India. That question is likely to become one of the dominant issues of the twentieth century, and it is certain in course of time to touch very nearly the most central interests of the British Empire. Our reply to it is very simple. We do not admit that the British sovereignty over India implies, for example, the unrestricted right of the people of India to flood Western Canada with their overspill. We do not accept Mrs Besant's apparent contention that Indians can claim admission to any English clubs, because clubs are founded upon a basis with which Mrs Besant, like many women, is still imperfectly familiar. The railway question will settle itself, and incidents of the nature which Mrs Besant indicates grow rarer every year. They could still be paralleled by many episodes which suggest that such very small restrictions as continue to obtain are not unwarranted. The fundamental characteristic of British rule in India, which Mrs Besant seems to question, is this. After centuries of internal strife, which inflicted untold hardship upon the peasantry, British rule has brought to India peace and prosperity. We recommend any inquirer who has doubts upon this point to read the records of the Deccan under the Peishwas. The advent of internal peace, and of a prosperity such as the predecessors of the present generation of Indian peasantry never knew, has brought with it a demand for self-government without such restrictions as still obtain. The wonder is, not that such a demand exists, but that it is not more insistent. The answer to all pleas of the kind advanced by Mrs Besant is that India has in recent years received a substantial enlargement of her share of government, and that the process cannot be accelerated without risk of a set-back. So long as the British Empire endures, Great Britain must and will bear the burden of responsibility which she has undertaken towards India It is well for India that she should do so; but we agree with Mrs Besant that the British control should be carefully exercised, and not unduly obtruded.

THE VOICE OF THE EAST

AN INDIAN LADY ON INDIAN AFFAIRS

(*The Times*, June 3, 1914)

To the Editor of *The Times*.

Sir,—Your leading article in *The Times* of May 30 has answered Mrs Besant very completely upon the emigration question, and on one or two other points. But her great gift of oratorical language is so misleading that no one acquainted with facts, and belonging to India, and living and working in India, is entitled to keep silence if there is even one further word which can be said to minimise the inflammatory nature of her statements.

Mrs Besant talks of the events of the last few years as "a rude shock to the belief that England loved liberty, and that when she saw political unrest she endeavoured to seek its causes and to remove them." And she then proceeds to abuse the Government of India for doing the very thing which she would have seemed to desire—viz., for seeking by its Press Act to control the misrepresentations, the distortions of truth, the incitations to anarchy which are undeniably the successful aims of one section of the vernacular Press in India. That is, Mrs Besant is blaming the Government for "seeking and endeavouring to remove" a very potent and insidious "cause of unrest" in India.

And as for the "events of the last few years," political liberty has surely never moved with quicker strides in any Empire. Indeed, there are those who fear that the large and rapid share given to Indians of late years in representative government in India may prove our own undoing; and that it is possible to put not too narrow but too liberal an interpretation on the word liberty —when you are speaking and acting "in English," in a country where the masses still speak and love the vernacular!

Is intimidation worthy of the advocates of "liberty"? Can Mrs Besant say that the people associated with the Government help in the repression of crime as they alone could help had they the mind? They boasted that the denial of demands made by the unscrupulous would lead to exactly the anarchical programme which has been carried out in India, and which is continued although these demands have been granted. And it is a little amusing that Mrs Besant should now be championing causes and methods with which she expressed herself wholly in disagreement at a time when she was asking financial help from Government for her Hindu College in Benares.

"Eastern Philosophy"

There are those who drug themselves with fragments of Eastern philosophy culled from American books, or written by Americanised Hindus clever enough to apply modern Western interpretations to age-old Eastern saws—and they send the hot blood to the head of Young India by talking of "the East having nothing to learn from the

West"; by boasting of a dead past, and making it the basis of claim to a present which that which was best and greatest in that past would never have sanctioned. The struggle to get rich, the desire to play the game of politics as played in England. Could the old Rishis, whose aim was to feel after God, and who even renounced kingdoms to go out into the forest and meditate if haply so, in silence and aloofness, they might find Him—could they have sanctioned Mrs Besant's plea for an unrestrained vernacular Press in all its violence and inaccuracy and incitation to rebellion? Could they have sanctioned any part of Mrs Besant's political programme? And yet, if Mrs Besant has any claim to a hearing at all, it would be not about politics or the present condition of India, but about the meditations in the forest of these same Rishis.

Equal privilege of service for India in what is considered the highest grades of that service has long been open to us—although many Indians have counted the cost (loss of caste and family and orthodox Indian social privilege) too great to pay for the liberty of visiting England and becoming a member of the Civil Service. What the discontented Indian now claims, and Mrs Besant for him, is really not equality but special privilege. He does not say, "Give me this because I have the same qualifications as an Englishman," but "Give me this because you must make allowances for me in not having the same qualifications." And he forgets that we do not "make allowances" for our equals, but for our inferiors.

The Indian had his traditions and ideals too, but he has forsaken them by the very act which has put him in competition with Englishmen in the struggle for place and power and wealth and temporal aggrandisement.

He forgets this, and the English students of half-digested translations of the Eastern spirit forget this also. The whole vocabulary of modern Indian demand is wrong—suffragist methods of aggression and intimidation grounded on Eastern claims to be the students of quiet and of the renunciation of the temporal! Should we not recognise such a sequence as impossible?

An Indian Ideal

I dream of an Empire into which every nation shall bring its own special glory and honour; and I would see Indians nursing the growing-pains of the transitional period of our history in silence and obscurity until that which the West has taught us has helped us to make the best use of our own national gifts and inspirations for the privilege of service.

Mrs Besant talks of social difficulties, and means apparently social intercourse with English folk. But there are far wider social issues than that at stake, and we need no charter from England to solve them. Our questions of custom, disastrous to health and to morals; our problems of the domestic "fire and water"—each Indian heart knows its own bitterness and difficulties about these. Then there are social problems between Indian and Indian. Mrs Besant refers to an age-old incident in a railway carriage between an Englishman and an Indian. It has often been quoted. But I have an entirely Indian railway-carriage scene to put beside that. And here it is. Time, present day; scene, Howrah railway platform, Calcutta. Punjab mail just about to leave. A Hindustani (old fashion) in loincloth is sitting in a first-class carriage, his hookah beside him. An "England-returned" Bengali comes up dressed in English clothes, pink shirt, patent leather shoes, bowler included; he finds that a berth in the Hindustani's carriage is the only one available on a crowded train. He is furious, and demands that the Hindustani should go elsewhere. The Hindustani says no word, simply holds out a first-class ticket which he has untied from a knot in his waist-cloth.

The Bengali sends for the guard, and demands that the Hindustani should be removed. The man is still holding out his ticket in silence.

The guard examines it. "Sorry, sir; you have not reserved the entire carriage; the other gentleman has a ticket. Time up, sir; train just off," and he blows his whistle.

The educated Indian's objection to the Hindustani is probably identical with the Englishman's objection in the oft-quoted story. He fears that the manners and customs of his travelling companion may not be the same as his own.

Would Mrs Besant not do more service to India in pointing out this simple fact (and its like in kindred misunderstandings) than in talking of rancour and bitterness, and quoting worn-out tales of the discourtesy of individuals ?—Yours faithfully,

CORNELIA SORABJI.

LONDON, *June.*

MRS BESANT AND INDIA

THE QUALIFICATIONS OF ENGINEERS

(*The Times*, June 5, 1914)

To the Editor of *The Times*

Sir,—The attention of this institution has been drawn to a letter addressed to you by Mrs Annie Besant in your issue of May 30, in which it is stated that "the Institute of Engineers demands higher qualifications from the Indian than from the English students."

The grounds for the statement are not given; and if, as is probable, the Institution of Civil Engineers is referred to, I am authorised to say that it is a matter of concern to the institution to observe such a suggestion of unequal treatment of those who seek the recognition it accords to professional engineering qualifications.

The qualifications for membership of this institution apply uniformly to all candidates for election into it; and, in view of the importance of that situation to the engineering profession, I trust you will permit me to correct the statement above referred to.—I am, sir, yours faithfully,

J. H. T. TUDSBERY,
Secretary to the Institution of Civil Engineers.

GREAT GEORGE STREET,
WESTMINSTER, S.W., *June 3.*

MRS BESANT AND INDIA

A REPLY TO MISS SORABJI

(Proof sent from *Times*)

To the Editor of *The Times*

Sir, — You will doubtless permit me to reply to Miss Cornelia Sorabji's letter in your issue of June 3, as some of her statements with regard to myself are inaccurate and her view of the teaching of the Rishis is very misleading, and is disproved by Indian literature. As regards myself, I object to the Press Act, because it was passed with the statement that injustice would be prevented by appeal to the High Courts; the High Court of Calcutta, lately appealed to, has said that the action of the Executive was "illegal," but that it was unable to interfere. It tries to suppress legitimate criticism, whereas such criticism is the safety of Government by drawing attention to abuses. It is used against Indian, and not against English editors, however abusive the latter may be, and however much they stir up hatred against the Indians. It is unnecessary, for incitements to murder and rebellion are punishable by ordinary law. The Indians are no more able to discover the authors or abettors of crime than are the police; the anarchists are the worst enemies of India, and Indians are at one with the Government in the wish to repress crime. I champion no causes and methods with which I disagreed when I "was asking financial help from Government for her Hindu college in Benares." I have opposed from the beginning, and oppose now, all political crimes and methods of conspiracy, and am denounced by Krishnavarma and his friends for this reason. I have never at any time asked for any financial help from Government for the Hindu College at Benares, but have relied entirely on voluntary support. Not one rupee has ever been asked for from Government nor given by it to the Hindu College.

The Hindu Rishis were particularly active

people in worldly affairs; they visited the courts of kings, questioned the rulers on all matters of government, on the wages of artisans, the seed supply of agriculturists, the support of the widows and orphans of soldiers. Has Miss Sorabji studied the long speech of Bhīshma on the duties of monarchs and of subjects? Has she read the Dharma Shastras, the Mahābhārata, the Rāmāyana, which all bristle with worldly affairs? Does she remember the objects of human life as laid down by the Rishis—the pursuit of "duty, desire, and wealth"? Has she read the prayers they taught the people, for riches, prosperity, power, progeny, victory over their enemies? The Rishis were law-makers, councillors of kings, statesmen, active interveners in public and national concerns. Life, by their rules, was divided into four periods—studentship, householder, retirement from public life, asceticism. During the household period a worldly life was commanded, power, rank, and wealth were to be sought. Men went to the forest and meditated, "renouncing kingdoms," only after they had enjoyed to the full the struggle for wealth and the activity of political life. They do so still. To renounce after full experience is the Hindu ideal. Miss Sorabji would have Indians renounce without experience. Moreover, it must be remembered that all great Indian literature belongs to the time of India's freedom, and that the revival of her literary power has come with the spirit of nationality. It is the Indian's "traditions and ideals" which have given birth to the new spirit, and if it throws him into competition with Englishmen, it is the Englishmen who have intruded into India and challenged the competition. To ask the people of a country to practise renunciation in order that the foreigner may enjoy, unchallenged, wealth and power therein seems a little audacious. The Indian asks for no special privilege, he complains of the special privileges enjoyed by aliens to his detriment. He does ask for equality, and is resolute to obtain it.

I have, unfortunately, though travelling constantly on Indian railways, never seen a man in a loin-cloth in a first-class carriage, nor a Bengali in a bowler hat. I have seen, and heard of from sufferers, very many insults to well-dressed Indian travellers.

I did not allude to any one "age-old incident," but to repeated insults known to every traveller and occurring every year. When the "discourtesy of individuals" ceases, we will cease to complain of it—not before. For each new case rankles in the Indian mind.

The difference of qualifications I alluded to for admission to the Institution of Civil Engineers was that the matriculation examination of any English university or of some colonial universities exempts from the studentship examination, whereas a student must have passed the degree examination of the Indian universities for a similar exemption. Also Rule A of Part 2, Rules of Examination, allowing a student of the institution to present himself at the end of a year for the Associate examination, is stated in *The Status of Indian Students in the United Kingdom*, pp. 11 and 12, not to be applied to Indian students, who must work for two or two and a half years before presenting themselves.

ANNIE BESANT.

PRESENT-DAY PROBLEMS

INDIA AND THE EMPIRE

By Annie Besant

(*The Nation*, May 30, 1914)

It is a remarkable comment on the curious indifference of England to her "great dependency" that, in all the discussions now rife on the question of the Federation of the Empire, India is quietly left on one side. There is no deliberate intention to do injustice; there is merely a vast ignorance. There is a general vague idea that India is a "conquered country," that she "is held by the sword," that she is more or less barbarous, and does not count when Imperial questions are to the front. People read, in articles on Census Reports in the daily Press, remarks on the hill-tribes and other savages who still remain ensconced in some of the recesses of her vast extent, and think, more or less casually, that these are "Indians." Obviously, these need not be considered when matters of self-governing nations are being discussed. Her people are "natives," "coloured," and the words call up pictures of Hottentots and Kaffirs, and others of that ilk. So the British nation blunders along after its wont, and is risking the loss of the noblest opportunity a people have ever had of building a world-Empire so mighty that it could impose peace on the world, and is tending steadily towards a war of "white" and "coloured," in which Asia, indignant at long exploitation and injustice, shall be pitted against Europe and America. It must not be forgotten that Japan's increasing population is beginning to press against her boundaries, and that Australia, with her sparsely settled lands, her ludicrously small five millions of white — rapidly tending towards yellow—men, and her unguarded thousands of miles of coast, offers a most tempting opportunity for colonisation, armed if necessary; only the Japanese Alliance with England and the floating

Union Jack over Australia defend that Asiatic country against invasion. Asiatic countries traditionally look to India as the land whence they have derived much of their civilisation, and already there are whispers in the Far East of what of good to the Asiatic world might happen if India should remember that she belongs to the East, not to the West. In the face of all this, with incredible and suicidal recklessness, the Colonies are treating the Indians as an inferior race, and are shutting them out—where they do not take them as indentured, *i.e.* as slave labour,—and Britain remains supine and shows herself unable to protect British subjects, while the United States jauntily remark that as Britain allows them to be shut out of her Colonies, she cannot complain if the American Republic follows suit.

Now, India does not desire to shatter her allegiance to the Crown, but she passionately desires the removal of the laws which cramp and fetter her: she demands self-government within the Empire, and she is resolute to win it. She is gradually developing a national self-consciousness, and the late troubles in South Africa have done much to quicken this; in her protest against the cruel injustice with which her children there were treated she felt herself as one. Meetings all over India voiced a single protest; all the various classes were welded together by a common emotion; women threw themselves into the stream of public feeling, money poured in at Mr Gokhale's demand —more than was needed. For the first time a thoroughly national demand was made, and India felt her own strength. She will never forget that by her own action she won a Viceroy's aid and redress for the worst wrongs under which her children laboured.

But she will never again tamely submit to exclusion from other countries, while those same countries claim the right to enter freely into India, and to flood India with their products. In Australia, in Canada, the immigration of Indians is now a burning question, and the resolution to fight it out is seen in the 600 Hindus who are invading Vancouver to insist on their right of entry. Foreigners have forced open by violence the doors closed against them by China, and the "open door" became a war-cry. Now colonists claim to keep their doors shut against British citizens. Will not Great Britain consider what Indians ought to do? If they are to be shut in within the limits of India, and to be denied the ordinary human right to travel freely in other lands, may they not fairly claim at least to have their own land to themselves, and to shut all white men out of it? Is it surprising that a murmur is making itself heard to shut out all Colonials? The resentment which is spreading is not the vocal resentment of the much maligned "educated class"; it is a dumb resentment, spreading among the masses of the peasantry, whose kith and kin it is who are refused an outlet for their industry. It will be ill for the Empire when this peasantry, feeling the ever-growing grievance of their exclusion from the right to win their bread, turn to their natural leaders, their educated fellow-countrymen, and cry to them for help. The Indian masses are neither loyal nor disloyal; they are indifferent to Governments, which, to them, from time immemorial, exist only to plunder them of their hard-won earnings. The only intelligent loyalty to the British Government in India is that of the educated classes; they desire self-government, but self-government within the Empire; England has taught them to love liberty, to admire free institutions, and they look to England to carry out in India all that she elsewhere declares is essential to national and individual self-respect. Their faith in her professions is shaken, but is not yet destroyed; they are still willing to be guided in their building-up of free institutions by the experience of the English, but they demand that the building shall proceed.

How is this educated class being treated? There is the Press Act, to which their consent was gained by a promise that the High Court would redress any wrong—a promise shown to be illusory. This Act is administered harshly against Hindus and Mahomedans, but is a dead letter when English-edited papers stir up hatred against Indians.

They have long asked for the separation

of executive and judicial functions, for the union of the two causes frequent injustice and spreads disbelief in "British justice." A "Collector" (magistrate), tired out with revenue work, listens impatiently to counsel, hurries his decisions, pays no attention to evidence, suddenly fixes a place of trial perhaps twenty miles away at his next camp, increasing the expenses of the litigants, putting lawyers, witnesses, and principals to most serious inconvenience, sometimes making the hearing impossible. Despite all urging, nothing is done, and the people despair of justice.

They ask for representation on the India Council, a modest third of the members to be elected by themselves. Will the prayer be granted? They complain that the ever-increasing cost of higher education is becoming prohibitory, and urge that the Education Departments should not, under pretence of efficiency, crush out schools which are at least better than nothing; but the Juggernaut car goes on relentlessly.

They ask that they shall not be barred out by colour only from posts in their own land; that regulations shall not be made which force their sons to qualify in England, and yet shut against them the colleges and other institutions where the qualifications are to be gained. They ask to be treated as political equals, and not as inferiors, in all branches of the Service. Government will find difficulty in staffing its Services with any but inferior men if the present *régime* continues, for the better type of younger men will not submit either to rudeness or to benevolent patronage. They feel themselves to be the equals of the white men, and see no reason why the white should treat them as inferiors.

They ask that in all the Services young Englishmen, just imported, shall not be put over the head of Indians who are efficiently performing their work. For example, a young man is brought over from England as professor, and placed over Indian assistant professors of far greater knowledge than he can claim. They resent their exclusion from clubs and the social treatment they receive, and they rightly feel that this will continue until political freedom is gained, and all posts in the Services are thrown open to them on the same terms as to Englishmen.

There is nothing in all this which borders on sedition, which deservedly causes suspicion and distrust. Nothing is more dangerous, more disloyal to the Empire, than the flouting of this splendid class of patriotic men, and the constant misrepresentation of their aims and conduct. For the sake of England, as much as for the sake of India, their co-operation and advice should be sought and welcomed; for the stability of British rule in India depends on them.

COLOUR BAR IN THE DOMINIONS

By Annie Besant

(*Daily Chronicle*, June 3, 1914)

The British Empire, growing into solidarity of feeling and endeavour, is seriously menaced in a way that no other nation, seeking for Empire, has to face. The majority of its people are coloured, the minority white. But the white claims not only to rule in white countries, but also to appropriate all the highest posts in the coloured countries, expropriating their own inhabitants, however highly civilised, however well educated, however capable the latter may be. It is "the white man's burden" to manage and improve them—after his own ideas. The Indians, at least, say among themselves that they find the white man himself a very serious burden on their coloured shoulders, and think that the burden is beginning to be greater than the benefit.

Anti-Indian Prejudice

While the white man claims to intrude himself and his goods into every coloured country, the coloured men are forbidden by him to enter the countries which he chooses to dub white, after he has taken them from coloured men of a savage type, Australian, Red American Indian, Kaffir, etc. The savages are wiped out sooner or later, for they cannot effectively resist; but the huge Indian peninsula is peopled by highly civilised races—leaving apart the aborigines remaining as hill tribes and the like—races of Aryan descent. The "white countries" shut these Indians out, and make various laws to effect their purposes; British Columbia says Indians may not land unless they come direct from India, and there is no direct line by which they can come.

Australia has a language test, adopted with Mr Joseph Chamberlain's approval, which enables the authorities to offer Russian or modern Greek as a test. South Africa is more frankly brutal. Australia deported the South Sea coolies who were raising its sugar-cane in a tropical climate. South Africa has used coolie labour to cultivate Natal, to work in mines, to improve the country. Now all the Colonies are rising against Indian immigration, on the general pretext that Indians lower the scale of living, and that white labour, demanding meat, intoxicants, and greater "comfort," cannot exist on the wages that keep Indians well fed and contented. It is useless to say that white men, in tropical countries, would be much healthier if they adopted a less stimulating diet; the uncultivated whites will not improve their ways of living, and no one has the right to impose improvement on them. The Indians are hated for their virtues, not for their vices, and it is true that they flourish where white men would starve. But have whites a divine right to colonise and usurp rule in tropical countries, and to exploit coloured people for their own benefit? They are practically re-establishing slavery, after England, at least, prided itself on its abolition.

The conditions in India which lead to emigration may be readily understood. Economic conditions have supplied the field which emigration agents have tilled, and with fair promises they have induced Indians to leave their own country to labour abroad; higher wages are promised than planters will give, and the factory life offered by manufacturers in large towns has no attraction for the agriculturists who for many generations have lived by tilling the soil. The conditions under which India flourished in the past have largely changed since the establishment of British rule, and life is no longer supported so easily as in past days.

India's Past Industries

It must not be forgotten that India in the past was a great trading country, exporting the goods produced by her flourishing handicrafts, as well as various valuable natural products. Her weaving industries were a mine of wealth; her silks, muslins, shawls, carpets, woven fabrics of every kind, were eagerly sought for; her workers in metals, her carvers in wood and stone, were renowned all over the civilised world. As Phillimore said in the eighteenth century, she was so wealthy that "the droppings of her soil fed distant regions."

Now her handicrafts have decayed; her weavers and dyers are disappearing into the agricultural class under the pressure of power machinery, Indian and foreign; her metal workers and artificers are starved out by cheap, vulgar, foreign-made goods, with which the country is flooded; railways carry away her food-stuffs; their embankments turn fertile land into malarial swamps. Village life is impoverished, and the peasants, attracted by the promises of emigration agents seeking cheap labour, leave their homes and become indentured labourers, exported to South Africa, the Fiji Islands, etc. Frugal, industrious, temperate, they save a little money, and become traders, when free from their indentures. Then the white colonists take alarm; they want their labour as coolies; they dread their competition as traders. Next, by exceptional laws, they try to get rid of them in this character: to keep them coolies, to deport them, or to tax them crushingly — anything to prevent their success.

The Indian Government has forbidden the export of indentured labourers to Natal, but has not touched voluntary emigration. Apart from agents' promises, many emigrate, allured by news of the success of relatives and friends in foreign lands, and their influx is arousing keen antagonism among white settlers already in possession, as in British Columbia now. Australia fears that, unless it excludes, the Pacific may become "an Asiatic lake," and it is said that the battle for the world's Empire will be fought out on the Pacific. If that be so, a far-sighted statesmanship would conciliate Indian feeling, so that the 300,000,000 of India may not learn to look to Japan with hope as they turn from Britain in despair. Australia may yet have to plead to India for protection against invasion, and she may yet cry to those for defence whom now she excludes from her sparsely populated lands.

The Right of Force

What is the right in the white skin, India is now asking, to take the lands of coloured people, and to exclude others from the lands which the whites then claim as their own? The right of force? But that is a dangerous claim in India, where 300,000,000 of coloured people face some thousands of whites. The right of brains? But Indians meet the English in England, and prove themselves to be equal with the whites, though examined in a tongue which is not theirs, sometimes even to be the superiors of the pick of English universities; coloured skins do not prove inferior brains, and some say that much of the trouble arises from the fear that coloured men may prove to be as good as white ones in every walk of life.

This question is arousing India as a whole, and that for the first time. Indians passionately assert their equality as a race, and deny that the colour of a skin should be a political and social disqualification. Individual superiority they are quick to recognise and to honour, but they resent a governing caste founded on colour. Local troubles in India Britain has faced before, but here a whole coloured nation is massing itself against white injustice; Britain cannot play off one party against another, for all parties are one on this question. The peasantry are roused against the colour bar, and the women are on fire. It is not the educated class alone which here is concerned, as in political questions; it is a whole nation which is on its feet, demanding for its men or women the elementary human right to move freely at their will.

In the Middle Ages peasants were serfs, bound to the soil; but never yet has there existed a whole nation of serfs, fettered to the ground on which it lives. If the Colonies try to create this unheard-of condition, they will goad India into a determination to force the question of self-government, so that she may defend herself against such aggression. They are pushing to the front the perilous problem of coloured versus white all the world over, a veritable Armageddon of nations.

Great Britain has more to lose than any other nation by an arousing of the coloured peoples against the white, and it is this which the Colonies are precipitating with an incredible recklessness. "This question of the treatment of Indians in South Africa," said Lord Ampthill, "is a test of our fitness to be an imperial people, the test of the fitness of democracy to deal with external affairs."

British Columbia and Australia are raising the same question, and seem to be intent on proving that they are not fit to be part of an Empire in which the coloured outnumber the white.

EAST AND WEST

THE COLOUR BAR IN INDIA ITSELF

(*Daily News and Leader*, June 5, 1914)

To the Editor

SIR,—Among the many causes which are working to widen the gulf between Indian and British sentiment, one of the most immediately dangerous is the antagonism which arises from difference of colour. . . . The uprising of the Sepoys in the middle of the last century was practically a local rebellion, and British rule was saved by the rallying round it of chiefs and troops who regarded it as useful to the country. Now the alienation is becoming general and the resentment national. Britain has ever held her Indian possessions with the assent of large numbers of the Indian chiefs and peoples. As the Moslem Empire was made possible by the quarrels of Rajput clans, so did internal dissensions render victorious the British invaders, and Lord Minto spoke the literal truth when he said: "When Indians do not want us, we shall have to go."

But Indians, the great majority of educated Indians, do want the British Crown to remain as the paramount Power; they value English education, the contact with Europe, the science and manufacturing facilities brought by British rule; they admire British energy, British institutions, and British freedom. They admire them so much that they want to imitate them. . . .

The great class of Sanskrit-educated Indians, deeply learned in their own classics, and men of high culture in the various branches of Oriental learning, stand wholly apart from the English-educated Indians in their thought and knowledge, and neither class exercises influence over the other. These, the Sanskrit-educated, want nothing from the English, look down upon them with haughty pride, the pride of thousands of years of scholarly descent, and care not for the invaders, successively Greek, Moslem, Christian, all turbulent crowds [seething round their quiet āshramas, coming and going, impermanent. We may leave this class on one side, as taking no part either for or against Government. Only on some religious question would they have power to rouse the people to frenzy].[1]

The Real Danger

The real immediate danger lies in the growing exasperation of the English-educated class against the political and social inferiority of which colour is the mark, the resentment aroused by the treatment accorded to them by an aggressive alien race, intruding into a civilised country and treating its people as inferiors on the mere ground of the colour of their skins. This sense of the skin-born superiority of the white man shows itself in abusive epithets and blows inflicted on the "natives," mostly, though not entirely,

[1] I am not sure if these are the exact words left out, but they are the sense of them. I am unable to remember either the words or the sense of the omitted passages in the first and second paragraphs.

by the rougher section of the white people, and by the light punishments inflicted for assaults on Indians, often ending in death. I have seen an Englishwoman come into a first-class waiting-room at a railway-station, and strike a coolie with an umbrella because he did not put down her luggage in the exact spot pointed out by her unintelligible Hindi. I have seen Englishmen kick coolies for a similar reason.

Indian gentlemen are so often insulted if they travel first-class that they often prefer to travel second. "All niggers here!" said a young civilian, putting his head into a railway carriage in which I was travelling at night with some Indian friends, my own face being turned away from the door. "No niggers wanted here," said a civilian to another friend of mine, who was entering a first-class carriage. Eurasians are employed as ticket-collectors and station-masters, and they show gross incivility to Indian travellers, while cringing to white. "Stop that row," said an Englishman to an Indian suffering from a bad cough, "or I'll throw you out of the carriage." The Indian drew a pocketknife—he was too weak to resist otherwise—and the Englishman subsided.

In many Indian stations bedrooms are provided to accommodate travellers for the night. An Englishman and an Indian were travelling together; they arrived at a station in the evening, and the Englishman asked for admission to a bedroom for himself and his friend. "You can go in, sir," was the answer, "but the native cannot." "But there are only two beds, and if I do not object, why should not my friend come with me?" "Against the rules, sir." Appeal to the station-master was useless.

The Widening Gulf

At stations where plague passports are issued, all Indians are turned out on the platform, though in the middle of the night, while the clerks go to the compartments in which there are white travellers. Everywhere these distinctions are made, and Indian gentlemen, in their own country, are obliged to submit to degrading distinctions, and to continual insults from ill-bred Englishmen. The result is a growing exasperation, especially among the younger men, a haughty courtesy in necessary official relations with Englishmen, and a bitter hatred hidden within the heart. The insults are remembered, the story of them constantly repeated, and the gulf grows wider.

Even the more highly placed Indians are not exempt from violence. Lately, in Madras, an Indian nobleman, fearing to miss his train, drove his car swiftly past an Englishman's. The Englishman followed him to the station, insulted him, struck him and kicked him so seriously that the Indian was lifted helpless into the train; he summoned the Englishman, and a paltry fine was inflicted. The ex-Sheriff of Bombay was assaulted as he approached a ladies' carriage to speak to his wife; he summoned his assailant; and the man apologised and was let off. Such cases are innumerable. Sentences of whipping for trivial thefts are constantly inflicted on coolies; and in one case recently, where a little tobacco was stolen by a railway coolie, he was sentenced to be flogged by a magistrate, and flogged in the magistrate's office by the magistrate himself, according to the testimony of several respectable Indians. The magistrate was "severely reprimanded," but remains on the Bench. A coolie, struck by his master, died; a fine was inflicted, as "there was only one blow, and it was not meant to kill." "You can kill an Indian for 25 rupees," one hears Indians say, "but if an Indian strikes a sahib . . ." I have lived among Indians as a friend for twenty years, heard their comments, noted the growing resentment, and wonder—how it will end. For the Indian is no longer passive, no longer submissive. His self-respect is constantly outraged, and he does not forget.

The political colour bar is, of course, more important than the social insults, but that will be gradually removed, and India is patient where reforms are being introduced. The social stings madden proud and sensitive men, and the exasperation they cause is an immediate danger, and people in England hear little or nothing of them. On the one side, there is an arrogant class, growing more and more angry as it watches the rising spirit of the Indians, a "subject race"; on the other side, an increasing, but mostly concealed, hatred, which is gagged by the Press Act and smoulders unexpressed. A significant phrase is often heard: "We must teach our boys to box."

ANNIE BESANT.

[*We add the following important letter from Lālā Lajpat Rai.*]

LAJPAT RAI AND BRITISH CITIZENSHIP

"A GREATER MEASURE OF SELF-GOVERNMENT"

(*The Daily News and Leader*, June 10, 1914)

To the Editor

SIR,—I wonder if Englishmen at home realise the full significance of the attempt of the Hindus aboard the *Kamagata Maru* to enter Western Columbia in exercise of their rights of British citizenship.

The first thing to note in connection therewith is that these Hindus are Sikhs, the descendants, compatriots, and co-religionists of those who saved His Majesty's Eastern Empire in the time of England's greatest peril in India, viz. in 1857.

But for the loyalty and the bravery of the Sikhs, one shudders to think what the fate of the Empire would have been. Possibly, nay probably, that Empire would have been lost. Then the Sikhs have shed their blood for the Empire in Egypt, in the Soudan, in China, in Abyssinia, and in Burmah, and it is from their ranks that a considerable part of His Majesty's Indian Army is recruited. Some of your best generals have called them the "flower" of the Indian Army. They have been, and are believed to be, above the taint of sedition, and any educated Indian supposed to be agitating among them receives the severest (sometimes the most summary) punishment which is in the power of the Government of India to inflict. The mere suspicion of such a thing as agitation among the Sikhs raises the direst anger of the British official in the Punjab, and justifies the harshest measures of repression, such as were adopted in 1907. Yet here we are on the threshold of a great agitation among the Sikhs, the responsibility of which cannot be traced, even by a stretch of imagination, to any "agitator."

Equal Rights

The fact is that the British Government in India is on the horns of a dilemma. They want the Indians to believe that they are the equal subjects of the King, but when the former claim their rights as such, they behave as if they have neither the power nor the desire to secure the same for them. Perhaps it is not so much the fault of the Government in India as of those statesmen who have to reconcile their professions and principles of Liberalism with their policy of subjection. There is no half-way house between democracy and despotism. So long as India is governed from Whitehall and is not free to retaliate, the difficulty with which the Government is face to face in Canada will not be removed. The desire, the ambition, and the necessity of claiming the rights of British citizenship is no longer confined to educated Indians, but is permeating through the uneducated classes and even the masses.

The unlimited competition of the foreigner in the trade and service markets of India leaves them no other choice. The Indian labourer has so far been exploited for the benefit of the British Colonies under the most degrading and humiliating conditions. It has, however, done him one good: it has brought him the consciousness of his value as a worker. But just when he awakes to this consciousness he finds that there is no room for him in the world. At home his wages are despicable, and he can hardly live a decent life on those wages. Even the Government sweats him; when permanently employed in Government offices his wages ordinarily range from 2s. a week to 4s. or 5s. a week. When skilled and educated, he finds that most of the good places are held by the foreigner. Every riff-raff of a European, not to speak of British Colonials, has free admittance into India, and a large number of German, Italian, French, and American mechanics and engineers find employment in Government establishments and industrial concerns, while a great many skilled Indians, some of them educated in the best technical institutions in India, England, and America, remain unemployed, or have to be contented with very inferior positions. He thus suffers doubly. His country is open to the competition of the whole world, while he is debarred from admittance even into parts of the British dominions. Is it a wonder that he has begun to complain that if he had a Government of his own at his back, the world would not treat him thus? He feels helpless and friendless.

Power of Exclusion

To my mind, the remedy lies in giving a greater measure of self-government to India, with full powers of excluding foreign labour to the same extent and in the same way as the other parts of his Majesty's dominions do. Short of this, nothing is likely to avail much, and the trouble may continue to grow and embarrass both the Government and the Indian patriot, as it is no less embarrassing to the latter than to the former. It disturbs the Indian nation-builder in his work, and puts an unspeakable strain on his loyalty and on his patriotism. It reduces his influence with the younger generation of his countrymen, and disables him from enforcing discipline and self-restraint in public life.

The spectacle of 400 Sikhs taking to hunger-strike in British Canadian waters is fraught with serious consequences, and is likely to have the most disastrous effect on Sikh loyalty. The telegrams from Canada show that some of them have already commenced talking bitterly. The retired Sikh soldiers already settled in Canada are also suffering under certain disabilities, the most important of which is imposed by the so-called "Continuation-journey Clause," which effectually debars their wives and children from entering Canada.

It is time, I think, for British statesmen to apply their minds seriously to the solution of the problem, or else the trouble may grow in gravity, and then it will be futile to blame the poor "agitator" for the consequences thereof.

LAJPAT RAI.

June 7.

THE INDIAN PROBLEM

LETTER FROM MR LAJPAT RAI

(*The Christian Commonwealth*, June 17, 1914)

[*The Times* having refused insertion to the following letter, we are asked to publish it, and gladly do so.]

Sir,—I wonder if you would extend to me the hospitality of your columns for a few observations on the letter of Miss Cornelia Sorabji that appeared in *The Times* of June 3. I do not propose to deal with her criticism of Mrs Annie Besant's letter, because that eminent lady is more than sufficiently strong and able to look after herself. What I am chiefly concerned with is Miss Sorabji's attack on educated Indians, based on her misreading of the Hindu Rishis. I wish she had not dragged the poor Rishis into the discussion, because to me she does not appear to have read them happily, if at all. Her letter leaves an impression that politics were quite outside the sphere of the old Rishis, and the present political struggle is opposed to their teachings, and that if the Indians were to follow the old Rishis they would retire to the forests and engage themselves in meditations, etc. She sneers at "the struggle for place, and power, and wealth and temporal aggrandisement," and holds that the Indian has forsaken his "traditions and ideals" by the very act which has put him in competition with Englishmen for these things.

Now, firstly, Miss Sorabji forgets that it is not the Indian who has put himself in competition with the Englishman *in India*, but it is the latter who has done so. The struggle is not of the seeking of the Indian, and to blame him for it is, to say the least, adding insult to injury. If Miss Sorabji is right in saying that the Indian has forsaken his "traditions and ideals" by this act, then the responsibility of forcing him to do so and of creating circumstances which led him to it is not his. Secondly, Miss Sorabji is not right in her reading of the Hindu Shastras in thinking that the struggle for "place, and power, and wealth, and temporal aggrandisement" is opposed to the teachings of the Hindu Rishis. Has Miss Sorabji never read Bhishma's celebrated discourse on politics, or Chanak's aphorisms? Has she never heard of Vidura? Again, then, what are the Dharma Sutras, and how does she explain the numerous prayers in the Vedas for power, for wealth, for progeny, and for victory? In fact, the chief glory of the ancient Rishis consisted in their having so comprehensively dealt with all the problems of life and death and the questions that arise out of them. The whole body of Dharma Sutras and Smritis deals with politics. The Rishis concerned themselves with the affairs of the world quite as much, if not more than with the life hereafter. Are we to understand that they were unconcerned with the troubles, misfortunes, and miseries of life, and took no notice of what happened to men, women, and children around them, and did not care as to who regulated and controlled and guided the lives of the people in the affairs of the world, and how? To my mind, that would be a great libel on the progenitors of our race, and, if that were true, they would not be deserving of that respect and admiration which Miss Sorabji has for them. The truth is, that there is no department of life about which the Rishis have not left thoughts, which are worthy of consideration and study at the hands of the best and the greatest of men in all times and in all ages. It is equally true that the ruling note of their teachings is that "the struggle for place, and power, and wealth, and temporal aggrandisement" should always be subordinated to and carried on in accordance with the dictates of Dharma, that it will not do for man to gain the sovereignty of the world if he thereby stands to lose his soul. Subject to this, they place no limitations on the aspirations of men. And surely it is not ignoble to aspire "for place, and power, and wealth, and temporal aggrandisement" if by righteous means, because I am sure, if it were so, Miss Sorabji would not be occupying the position she does under the Government of India.

I am not a follower of Mrs Besant, nor have I always agreed with her in her views on politics or religion, but I must say that to me she seems to have a better right to speak of Indian wants and aspirations, by the mere fact that by the nature of her work she has come in the past, and daily comes, into contact with a larger number of Indian men, women, and children than Miss Sorabji could have ever done. Mrs Besant may be right or wrong in her views on Indian politics, but anyone with a grain of common-sense in him or her can find out that the Indian problem would not be any nearer solution if approached in the spirit of Miss Sorabji's letter.

The fact that Miss Sorabji was compelled out of a sense of duty to her Motherland to write this letter to *The Times*, proves that her ideal of seeing "Indians nursing the growing-pains of the transitional period of their history in silence and obscurity" is impracticable and unnatural. The world is too human to allow that, and I hope, sir, you will agree with me in this.

I cannot finish this letter without recording an emphatic denial of Miss Sorabji's assertion that in his political demands the educated Indian does not claim equality, but special consideration or "allowances," to use Miss Sorabji's expression. The Indian wants nothing but justice. In fact, for some time to come he might be contented with something less than equality.—Yours truly,

LAJPAT RAI.

INDIA, A BUTTRESS OR A PERIL?

MRS BESANT'S CRITICISMS OF BRITISH RULE

[*The Daily Chronicle* of June 12 was the only London paper that gave anything that could be called a report of the above lecture, although the great Queen's Hall was filled, and the audience was enthusiastic. *The Manchester Guardian* gave a fairly good report. We append that of *The Chronicle.*]

A LARGE audience assembled last night at Queen's Hall, to hear Mrs Besant on the grievances of India. Lord Brassey occupied the chair.

Mrs Besant said one heard little of the difficulties and troubles of the people of India, unless, like herself, one had lived years in the country, and were in close touch with

Indian friends. Indians admire England and might love her too, if she would only let them. For the first time in history the vast Indian population has been aroused by a question of the outer world, by Indian emigration to other lands. England can only hold India if her rule be just and intelligent.

The party of anger and anarchy is small, but the party suffering from the recent repressive measures is large, filled with righteous discontent; it is willing to go slowly, but demands that progress be made.

Dealing with the Press Act of 1910, Mrs Besant showed how severe it is. All but two Indians in the Council voted for it, but its repeal is now demanded.

Men, the lecturer said, have been deported and imprisoned, honourable gentlemen have been arrested and thrown into prison without trial.

Mrs Besant touched on the great frequency of flogging as a punishment by certain judges and collectors, and declared that the whole Indian criminal law needs revision. Our administration of justice was not so much admired in India as we are apt to suppose.

Indians are driven out of South Africa, Australia, New Zealand, British Columbia, but they must not also be shut out of posts in their own country. India must govern herself; she begins to realise her strength. England must live up to her old traditions and share her birthright with 300,000,000 Indians, for the price of Indian loyalty is the gift of freedom.

INDIA'S PLEA FOR JUSTICE

SHALL INDIA BE A BUTTRESS OR A MENACE TO THE EMPIRE?

(A Lecture delivered on June 11 in Queen's Hall, London)

EARL BRASSEY, who presided, said: In taking the chair this evening, I desire briefly to explain my position. I am here to ask for an attentive hearing for the address which Mrs Besant is about to deliver on the difficult question of unrest in India. Mrs Besant has spent many years in that country. She has lived in close relation with educated Indians. She is acquainted with their views and their aspirations. It is well that we should know what they are, and resolve, in so far as it may be possible, to meet them. As you will doubtless hear from Mrs Besant, the demands are many. There are grievances which it may be possible at an early date to remove. Take, for example, the demand for further rewards for good service under Government. To do what is required, changes of an organic character would be necessary, and these could only be gradually carried out. We may look for opportunities in connection with the great work of education. There are grievances keenly felt in India with which it is not possible for the Imperial Government directly to deal. There is bitter complaint that emigrants from India are not freely admitted into the self-governing dominions of the Empire. We have long since surrendered control of the local affairs in those vast and distant countries. We may represent our views; we cannot enforce them. And now, having recently—though not for the first time—visited India, it is my duty to bear testimony to the earnest desire of those filling positions of the highest responsibility to promote by all possible means the well-being and the happiness of the people committed to their charge. The Viceroy, at the head of the Government, my near relative who fills the post of Governor of Bombay, the officials at the head of the various branches of administration, are all in full sympathy with every legitimate aspiration. Looking nearer home, the sentiments of the people of Great Britain are those of the sincerest goodwill, coupled with a profound sense of the duty we owe to our Indian fellow-subjects. I must not pursue or stand longer between Mrs Besant and an impatient audience.

Mrs Besant:—My Lord Brassey; Friends: Probably only few among you keep in any sense in close touch with the vast Empire of India. Telegrams come to you from time to time telling of one event or another. You hear when there is any disturbance; you hear when some officer of police is unhappily murdered; you hear of any kind of outrage that occurs; news of these unfortunate events flashes across the telegraphic wires and rings through the country by your newspapers. But you do not hear of the many difficulties that surround the Indian people; you do not hear of the many troubles that press upon them, sometimes troubles that are well-nigh intolerable; you know nothing of the hopes frustrated, nothing of the aspirations beaten back, nothing of the desire to find in England a friend and a helper, a desire too often failing in its results, largely by mutual misunderstanding. Unless you take the trouble to have Indian papers sent to you, you cannot come closely into touch with the thoughts, the lives of the people themselves. And if I venture to put before you this evening what I have called "India's Plea for Justice," it is because for more than twenty years I have found my home, my friends, my dearest work, in the service of India, the mighty Motherland of the Aryan peoples, and amongst her children I have found, and find, many of my dearest and most trusted friends.

Now, in India to-day, as in the whole of Asia, changes are going on so rapidly that it is well-nigh impossible to keep in direct contact with them, unless your attention is constantly directed in order to see and trace them one by one. If a man goes back there five or ten years after he has left, he finds the whole atmosphere changed. Especially is this change found among the younger generation, those who are just finishing their college career, those who are just entering upon manhood's life, from about perhaps the age of eighteen to the age of five-and-thirty. You will find concentrated in those a very large part of the forward movement of India. The elder men have struggled against apathy, against inertia, and have constantly found their most splendid efforts failing against the mass of dead-weight impossible to overcome. One day Mr Gokhale, that greatest of Indian leaders, who is laying a shattered health on the altar of the country that he loves, speaking of the work of the elders in India, used one, I think, of the most splendid of phrases: "Others," he said, "hereafter shall have the happiness of serving India by their successes; we have the honour of serving India by our failures." It is to the hero who serves by failures, to the elders of India, to the founders of the Congress movement, to the men who in the midst of darkness have never despaired of the light, that all the younger ones should look with admiration and with reverence; for the younger will reap what these men have sown, and by the difficulties and the sufferings they have conquered, the redemption of India shall be wrought out.

But in the younger men, remember, you see the men with whom you will have to deal in the coming morrows of India, full of enthusiasm, full of passion, having learned from their study of English history many a lesson of liberty and ordered freedom, hoping to find in England one who will encourage all their most ardent aspirations, willing to be guided by England if she will lead them along the road of freedom. As one of them said to me but a few months ago: "We admire the English; we would love them if they would let us do so." But there lies the difficulty. The love they would give is conditioned by England's treatment of them, and their love of England is less than their love of liberty—as, indeed, it ought to be, for only those who are lovers of liberty can be relied upon for character and for work. Now the educated class, as it is called, in India is, of course, a minority, a small minority of the Indian nation. Generally in India we say the English-educated class, because there is a vast educated class in India, you must remember, the Sanskrit-educated class, who have enormous influence in matters of religion, and also over the great mass of the population if ever a religious question should arise; but they take practically no interest in the political and social problems of the day, save to oppose them where social reforms thwart some of their cherished ideas. England cannot look to that learned class either for advice on Indian problems or for help in Indian difficulties. Nor can England look to the great mass of the population: they are ignorant, moved by tradition and habit; they care nothing for the changes of the Government; they are interested in village questions; they are interested in the number of their cattle; they are interested in the weather, whether it be fair or foul for the crops; they are interested in the sons' and daughters' marriages, in the many questions that affect the village life; but until quite lately they have been absolutely indifferent to questions of government. To them the Government is only a machine for taxing them and taking away part of their hard-earned produce. And whether it be Mogul, or Portuguese, or Frenchman, or Englishman, it is always the demand for the tax; that is all they know of the Government. Sometimes people talk about the loyalty of the Indian masses. Let me tell you, there is no such thing in the Indian masses as a loyalty you can rely upon; they are ignorant, remember; they are not trained to understand any question outside the interests of the village. In the village they are shrewd, capable, able to judge. India is essentially a self-governing country, but the unit of government is the village, not the State; and it is in the village self-government will have to be founded, by the restoration of the village councils which from time immemorial have had the welfare and the prosperity of the village in their hands. But, meanwhile, until education spreads, until self-government is begun in the villages where all the people understand the questions far better than anyone else, until then you must rely for your Empire in India on the loyalty of the educated classes. They may be small in number, but they make the public opinion of India. To them the masses will look, not to the English people, when questions arise that touch them to the heart. And if you want to realise that, you have to understand that for the first time a large part of the population is beginning to be moved by something outside itself, by the question of emigration, by questions of settlement in foreign lands, where sons have gone out and sent back news to father and mother. There the awakening of the population is beginning. But as they awake they look to their own people, they look to their own leaders, and for the first time, by that question of South Africa, which is only part of the great problems that have to be solved, the masses of India have been moved by a question affecting the outer world, and they have followed the lead of the educated classes and have made their voice heard in their support.

Those educated classes are almost always spoken ill of in this country; they are said to be disloyal; they are said to be seditious; they are said to be the dangerous people for whom you want Press Acts, for whom you want deportation, for whom you want the many methods of despotism that are disgracing the name of free England throughout India to-day. But they are your only hope in India; on them depends the stability of British rule; on their agreement and their sympathy your Empire must be based. And if you cannot win them—and they are so easy to win; if you cannot hold them—and they are so willing to be held if only you will be just; if you cannot win them by the justice and by the beneficence of your rule, then I ask you who call yourselves free men in your own country—have you any right to hold them unless you hold them by love, by service, and by understanding? Their loyalty is the only intelligent loyalty in the country; win them, and you win everything; but you must win them by fair treatment, and not in any other way. And you are alienating them to-day as they have never been alienated from England since first England herself took over the rule of India.

Think for a moment of that great Proclamation of the dead but reverenced Queen, when, after the war of 1858, the Imperial Crown took authority and responsibility in

India: "It is our further will that, so far as may be, our subjects, of whatever race and creed, be freely and impartially admitted to office in our service, the duties of which they may be qualified by their education, ability, and credit duly to discharge. In their prosperity will be our strength; in their contentment our security; and in their gratitude our best reward."

So spake Victoria. For fifty-six years time has rolled on since those noble words were spoken, and if you find discontent and unrest, what becomes of the security whereof she spake, "the contentment which is our security," that contentment that British statesmanship should strive to secure?

Now, why is it that this country is in a condition of unrest? You may divide the unrest, as Lord Minto very wisely did, into two: the unrest of mere anger, which is slight and represented by the party of anarchy, very small and unsympathised with; then the righteous discontent which everyone who is educated into a love of freedom, as you have educated your Indian fellow-subjects, must inevitably feel so long as freedom is not within his reach, and he finds himself unfairly repressed by measures unjust and cruel. That righteous discontent will only be entirely removed when India possesses self-government within the Empire, and of that you need not have any doubt. They are willing to go slowly, but they must *go*; they are willing to grow into it wisely and carefully, but you must let them *grow*. And there are some things that you ought to abolish without any further delay. Now, the first of these—for I am going to speak to you quite frankly—is the Press Act of 1910. That Act was passed in a moment of panic, and it bears all the marks of its evil parenthood. Moreover, it was passed, you must remember, with the assent of all the Indian members of the Imperial Legislature except two. Lately Mr Surendanath Banerji proposed certain amendments in the Press Act. The Government would not grant them, and every Indian unofficial member except two voted for the amendments and against the Act that three years before they had voted for. Now, why was it? Why so strange a change? Because, when they voted for it, they believed that the Government was obliged to ask for it, facing a pressing danger, and because they were assured by the law member, Mr Sinha, that no real injustice could happen, because there was an appeal to the High Court against any possible unfairness by the Executive, and the law would defend them if any injustice were done.

Now that has proved to be absolutely an illusion. A case was brought lately before the High Court, and the High Court of Calcutta (the most independent of all the High Courts of India and the one most trusted by the Indian people) declared itself powerless to redress the wrong, declared that there was no redress to be given by the law where the Executive had struck a pamphlet or a paper, and pointed out that it was impossible for them to interfere, and that what the unfortunate defendant had to do was a thing practically impossible to do; to show, not that the words that he used could not be brought under the sweeping clause of "causing disaffection and discontent," but that by no possibility of construction of metaphor, or of image, was it possible that the words should arouse any feeling of anger.[1] Now, that is clearly an impossible thing, and the result of that decision of the High Court has been to join all the educated Indians together in a demand either for sweeping amendment or repeal—which is what they ought to have.

Think for a moment what the Press Act means. Since it was passed in 1910 there have been more than 800 prosecutions under it, of which more than 200 are prosecutions of newspapers.[2] You might expect that all

[1] "It is not enough for the applicant to show that the words of the pamphlet are not likely to bring into hatred or contempt any class or section of his Majesty's subjects in British India, or that they have not a tendency in fact to bring about that result. But he must go further, and show that it is impossible for them to have that tendency, either directly or indirectly, and whether by way of inference, suggestion, allusion, metaphor, or implication." —Sir Lawrence Jenkins, J. The High Court held that the forfeiture was illegal, but that it had no power to redress the wrong.

[2] 807 cases, of which 237 were newspapers. The Hon. Mr Bhupendranath Basu declared that "the law is a source of great peril, that is, against the spirit of the British Constitution, that it is derogatory to the self-respect of a nation—of a people, if you will, which is fast developing its self-consciousness."

of the things coming under a Press Act would have to do with the Press, but that is not really so. Under the Press Act come a number of other restrictive enactments. If a place is proclaimed you must not hold any political meeting there without the permission of the Executive. You must not hold a meeting of more than twenty people without police permission. You must go to the police and ask if you may be allowed to lecture. But those are Russian methods; they are not English. England has always told Russia that if she found it necessary to repress, then she ought to look for the causes which gave rise to the necessity and remedy the causes, and not try to silence the people who were crying out from their pain. We have always said that, with the most self-righteous hypocrisy, to all the countries of Europe that have ever practised these methods of oppression—Austria, Germany, Russia, Italy. We have lectured them all on the proper way of dealing with popular discontent, how we ought to remove the causes, how we ought not to blame the people who cry out. If you tread on a man's toe he is apt to cry out and to say that you are hurting him; but in India you expect to tread on the toes of all the people, and yet that they shall not emit a single cry of pain. And there lies the difficulty. The safety of the Government lies in knowing what hurts the people. If you prevent them expressing their view of the things that hurt them, you will inevitably have hatred and sedition instead of open and honourable protest.

Now every newspaper lies under the fear of the Press Act. Personally I have never been asked for security, but then I am in a white body, and that makes a wonderful difference in India. But I live in dread—well, I won't say dread, because it is not in my line, but in expectation—of being called upon to furnish it, because I know if what I print in *The Commonweal* were printed in some of the journals edited by some of my Indian friends, they would very soon find their security not only asked for but forfeited, and probably their Press forfeited too. We are all in danger of that, we Indian journalists, excepting if they be Anglo-Indians.

They are quite safe. Never yet, under any kind of provocation and abuse of educated Indians, of stirring up hatred of them in the minds of others, never yet has one of those papers been prosecuted. They are safe.

Now, how does it work? Suppose a new man comes into your printing office as manager; you must at once go and report it to the magistrate, and he may like to put security on you because of your new manager. If you want to move your printing press from one place to another, you must go and ask permission of the magistrate. Lately a small religious paper[1] that had existed for some time at a town called Wai, in the Bombay Presidency, wanted, for the convenience of printing, to move the press from Wai into Bombay; when, according to the Press Act, the owner went to ask permission to move it, 1000 rupees was demanded from him as security, not because the same man is not going to print it, the same people going to issue it, but merely because they wanted to

[1] *The Dharma,* devoted to religious, philosophical, and social topics. The High Court could not interfere, as "the magistrate was entitled to exercise his discretion."

move the press. That killed the paper; he had not got the thousand rupees.

Take another case, that of a Mussulman. A Christian missionary in the Punjab had made a very violent attack upon the Mussulman religion. The Mussulman had no redress, because that is allowed to the goose which is not allowed to the gander, and very foolishly this Mussulman gentleman wrote an answer in his newspaper. The result was that at once the Executive came down upon him and forfeited his security. He pleaded he had only answered when his religion was attacked, but he did not realise that one man might attack but the other man must not reply.[1]

And I might go on and give you dozens, scores, of cases like that. The field is so wide I can only point to one or two cases under each head to show you that I am not exaggerating, and then pass on.

Now take one point that is interesting in regard to this. It was a paper edited by a

[1] *The Abl-i-Hadio* of Amritsar. The Mussulman's writings "injured the religious susceptibilities of Christians." But what of those of the Mussulman?

Mussulman. You have probably heard of it, *The Zamindar*. The beginning of that trouble was the forfeiting a security of 2000 rupees for an article that was said to be seditious. I have read it, and there was not an atom of sedition in it; if I remember rightly, it was only some criticism of England's policy towards Turkey. Then after that the man, being a brave man, thought he would start again. 10,000 rupees' security —the highest allowed—was asked for before he was allowed to start. He went on with his 10,000 rupees' security, and the next step was to forfeit that, and also to forfeit the press.[1] So that within a few months 27,000 rupees' worth had been taken from that editor, and his paper for the time destroyed. He cannot have been very bad, because when a little later he asked to be allowed to restart his paper, they only put 2000 rupees' security on him for the third time. That now is being started, and we shall see how long it lasts.

These are the kind of things that are going on all the time in India, and, as I tell

[1] Worth 15,000 rupees.

you, during the three years more than two hundred papers have come under this, as well as five hundred other cases in which prosecutions under the Press Act have taken place. Realise what that means of irritation, of anger, of a feeling of unfair suppression of thought, and then you will know one reason for the growing unrest. The shutting out of fair criticism and the constant dread of being involved in prosecution injures the Press, and makes it less outspoken and less honest than it ought to be. A free Government should learn from a free Press, and not be afraid that the people should speak out that which they desire to have.

Then remember that that is not the only form of autocratic interference with the liberty of the subject that you have. Another thing that has been done fairly often is deportation and imprisonment without trial. I assure you I am not telling you of what goes on in Russia; I am telling you of what goes on in India. You remember, when nine men were deported from South Africa, what a fuss you made over it here. And yet those men were deported in the midst of a danger of civil war. But with us, harmless men like my friend Lajpat Rai, who is here, are deported or imprisoned without trial. He was seized and deported; they could not try him, because there was no evidence; all that he had said was in print, and I read it and am willing to read every word of it in any country in the world. But there is no proof wanted if you are not brought to trial; there is no defence wanted if you are put in gaol and kept there as long as the Government likes to keep you. And a number of my friends in Calcutta, honourable gentlemen, who never desired resistance to the British Government, were suddenly seized, arrested in their homes, carried away, and thrown into gaol without trial and without evidence. And even their wives for weeks were not allowed to know what had happened to them. They were lost to their families. These are the things, remember, that are going on in India, and are making people so bitter and so resentful. And we ask for the abolition of that old statute by which men can be deported or imprisoned without trial and without any evidence being given against them; for if you have no evidence to convict, you have no right to put the penalty of imprisonment or exile on any one.

There is another old Act I should like to see abolished, though I am not sure whether my Indian friends will quite back me up in that. I think the Arms Act ought to go. The Arms Act at present works in rather a curious way. The honest people do not bear arms; the thieves do. And so the thieves —dacoits, as we call them in India—are able to break into people's houses, beat them, sometimes murder them, and *they* find no difficulty in getting arms in spite of the Arms Act; so the mischievous people get them, but the honest people, who try to obey the law, are left helpless against armed aggression. Now the right to carry arms is the sign of a free man, and it is an insult that they are not allowed to carry them. They do not want to go about, as men do in America, with a revolver in the hip-pocket, always ready to shoot. I don't know of any of my Indian friends who want to show off in that way; but if you cannot trust the

Indian, after these last fifty-six years of patient constitutional working, if you cannot trust him, why do you expect *him* to trust *you*?

Now let us pass from these Acts which ought to be swept away—the three of them at least,—and let me take certain points of grievance very bitterly felt in India. First, with regard to education. Some of you may know that we do not feel very grateful to Lord Curzon, the late Viceroy, for his Education Act, for though that claimed to make things more efficient, and though the usual plea of the Government is that they are working for efficiency, it is better to have inefficient schools than none at all; and the Indians are beginning to complain of the effect of the present Government's policy of shutting up a mediocre school and leaving them with none at all, under the plea of an efficiency which ought to be grown into gradually and not demanded suddenly, especially in a poor country such as India is.

But apart from that question of the harshness of the way in which the University Act and the Education Departments work, I want to put to you one or two other points which you will at once recognise mean very unfair pressure upon Indian educationists. We have there the Deccan Educational Society which has done wonders for education, and contains some of the most learned and best educated Indians in the whole country. Dr Bhandarkar I may mention as one of them. All the members of that society were called upon to pledge themselves, not only that they would not oppose the Government, which was an unnecessary impertinence, but that not one of them would criticise any action of the Government. Surely that was going rather far. At least, a man might be allowed to criticise, if he might not be allowed to do anything else. And that kind of pressure is put upon all our school teachers, schoolmasters, professors, and principals, except, of course, where they wear a white skin; and then things are very different, as you will see in my next case.

There were three lecturers appointed in Calcutta University, one of whom was very hard-working in the Turkish Red Cross Society, and collected a large amount of money to send to his co-religionists to help them in the late war in the Balkans. They took interest in politics, but no one pretended to say that they were seditious, revolutionary, or anything else; in fact, until now the Mussulman has been the pet child of the Government, and always held up to those wicked Hindus as showing how loyal an Indian can be. But now they say that the Government will not confirm the appointment of those three lecturers, because we ought to have a "pure atmosphere of study" in the University, and we should not introduce any political feeling at all. And then the principal of a Punjabi college wrote a novel called *Sri Ram, Revolutionist*, and he put his hero into the well-known Gurukula of Hardwar, an admirable school belonging to the Arya Samaj, and there he said that he was trained in sedition. He is still principal of the college, and "the pure atmosphere of study" and learning is allowed to remain under his care, while the unfortunate professors were turned out, though they had written no novels untrue and libellous, they had made no speeches attacking the Government nor slandering anyone. Can you wonder if people put the two things together and say, "Why should the author of *Sri Ram*," who is an Englishman, remain a principal, while these three Indian gentlemen are turned out from the places the University gave them because they sympathised with their co-religionists in other lands? Why that was done we have never been able to find out, but a curious Nemesis came almost immediately on the Chancellor of the University—the Viceroy, who in most things is sympathetic with Indians—from the Vice-Chancellor, an Indian, who was very indignant at the way the professors had been treated. He had, under his duty, to confer the degree of Doctor of Law on a very eminent Russian,[1] who had been turned out of his professorship at Moscow because his views were not identical with those of the Russian Government, who then came to England and received a post at Oxford University in England, and then went to India on a visit. The Calcutta University bestowed a sign of honour upon the Russian

[1] Professor Uinagradoff.

revolutionary, although the Calcutta gentlemen were all turned out for their interest in political life. And one wonders what the Vice-Chancellor thought, and the Chancellor. The Vice - Chancellor did make some rather ironic remarks, only restricted by his innate good breeding from being a direct reproach. And all the world in Calcutta laughed, and wondered what was coming to education.

But let us take more serious matters than this. Take the question of the treatment of professors in Government colleges. You find a young man, fresh from the university, a young Englishman, brought over to a college and put over the heads of all the Indian seniors, who remain as assistant professors, while he is made professor over their heads.[1] Do you think they do not feel that, when they are thus superseded in their own country and among their own people? No post in the higher educational service[2]

[1] The Government of Behar imported an Englishman as Professor of History over the head of Mr Jadurath Sircar, whose historical work is well known.

[2] The Imperial Educational Service.

is open to any Indian unless he comes over here for his education. The Imperial Service must always have England as the door into it for English and Indian alike. However educated a man may be, however brilliant his degrees, however splendid his qualifications, unless he has come over here to one of your universities he is obliged to remain in the Provincial Service, with smaller pay and different social position. And the Educational Service is not the only one where that difficulty is found. In a moment I will mention the others to which the door is only open on English soil.

Pass from that to the treatment of students. This is a thing that raises very, very bitter feelings in India. You will truly say it is the fault of individuals, but it has largely been endorsed by the Education Department. For instance, there were two or three little boys walking along the road who shouted out to an Inspector, "Sahib, salaam, salaam!"[1] The Inspector got very angry; the tone was not nice! Why, when I go through a village they often shout out to me, and I always pat

[1] Mr Stark, Acting Inspector, Burdwan.

their heads. The children do not mean any harm. But the Inspector was very angry and took their names, and one of them, a little lad of thirteen, was sentenced to be flogged; and not only to be flogged publicly before all the others, but, in addition to that, when the father appealed to the Department, the boy's name was ordered to be sent out with the record of his flogging to every school in Bengal. That is the sort of thing that causes bitterness. It is these cruelties that stir up anger. The father took the boy away before he was flogged, but that did not make the feeling any the less bitter.

In another case some children, accustomed to pick flowers anywhere for a festival in one of the temples, went into a garden belonging to a police inspector. They ran away when he came out, but he sent the police after them, and they were arrested. One or two were caught and flogged, one of them in the presence of himself *and his wife*, and another (a little boy of twelve years) was bound over to be of good behaviour for a year and to keep the peace! I know you do not hear of these things in England, but these are the things that make so much bitterness and anger. And that tendency to brutality, and to the use of force, is one of the things that you have to think over in dealing with this question of discontent.

Then remember that criminals, petty criminals, grown men, are flogged for small thefts in India. A man the other day stole an ounce or two of tobacco from a train; he was a railway coolie; and he was sentenced to be flogged[1] and taken into the magistrate's office, and several Indian gentlemen stated that the magistrate, a Mr Sykes, administered the flogging himself. A question was asked in the Legislative Council, but their testimony was thrown away and Mr Sykes' word accepted that he had not himself flogged the man. It was clear that the flogging took place in the magistrate's office, and in his presence, without a doctor being present. At the inquiry it came out that the same magistrate had given four or five sentences of flogging on younger criminals, and had inflicted the

[1] Twenty-five stripes. He came out limping and shrieking with pain.

floggings himself. He is still on the Bench, having received a "severe reprimand." The reprimand he ought to have had would have been to have been sent away to do some other work, for you ought not to allow magistrates to take the execution of their sentences upon themselves in that brutal way. Then, take what is sometimes called British justice. We call it Anglo-Indian justice, because it is so different from the justice that you have over here. It is a big subject, and I can only point you to just one or two things in it. In the first place, in the High Courts you often find conviction given on insufficient evidence. Only lately, in Madras, a man was sent from court to court, and sentenced to death in each court. They refused stay of execution when he asked for it on very good grounds. He had to spend 5000 rupees in telegraphing the judgment over here in order to get a stay of execution. The Privy Council granted it; later, at the hearing, the Privy Council declared he was convicted on evidence that never ought to have been admitted, and advised the English judge to read the Evidence Act—a fairly strong rebuke to the judge. But, remember, that if that man had not been rich, he would have been hanged before the Privy Council had reversed his sentence. The question was raised over here in Parliament, I believe, but not pressed so far as it ought to have been.

The whole Indian criminal law needs to be revised and these punishments of flogging swept away. It is bad enough when used for crimes of violence; it is abominable when used for petty thefts. And yet if you look at the records of whippings of full-grown Indians, you will see how numerous they are.

There was another man in the United Provinces[1] who was condemned, stripped of his decorations, imprisoned, and after he came out of prison—having appealed and been refused a stay,—after having served the whole of his sentence, the Privy Council reversed the whole thing. But the man had served the sentence; he was outcasted by it; his life was ruined. All because it is not the habit in an Indian court to give stay of execution.

[1] Mr Chandhuri Nasar Ali Khan, an Oudh Talukdar.

I nearly went to gaol myself because of not being able to get stay of execution, though given permission to appeal on a "substantial ground of law"; and if it had not been possible to telegraph to the Privy Council, who at once granted stay, I might have been sent to gaol for not obeying an order which the Privy Council, on the hearing, declared I could not obey without bringing myself into conflict with English law, and that for an order which, it said, no court ought ever to have issued.

You cannot wonder under these circumstances that British justice is not as much admired in India as you are inclined to think it is admired, for I know that it is one subject of great self-congratulation over here. There is no difficulty about British justice over there, you have sometimes said. But every Indian reformer agrees in asking for the separation of the administrative and judicial functions. Understand that it means this: the magistrate, or collector, collects revenue, and he goes round to village after village gathering in the revenue; and that is all right. But when he is tired out with collecting revenue, he has also to do the proper judicial duties of a magistrate, and to try suits in that particular place. I have heard Indian lawyers give an account of their own experiences under this system. One of them said that while he was pleading a case before a magistrate, the magistrate was making up his accounts and did not listen. In another case, in the middle of the case, the magistrate went on to the next village, twenty miles off, to collect revenue, and the villagers, witnesses, and lawyers had all to go trailing off for twenty miles in order that the case might be finished.

It is quite true that when you get two Indians against each other an Englishman will often give an impartial decision between them. But the main difficulty arises when the quarrel is between English people and Indians, and no justice is done in those cases —quite apart from this particular grievance of having to follow a peripatetic magistrate about, or to plead before a magistrate who does not listen to you while you are talking, and sometimes has even written his judgment before he has heard the counsel for the defence. Apart from that—for the justice of that charge is admitted, although it is not carried out—there are other points that you have to remember. Where a quarrel between an Englishman and an Indian comes before a court of law, and a blow has been struck on either side—and the blow mostly comes from the Englishman, not often from the Indian, I am sorry to say, in return—I wish that every Indian boy should be taught to box, for then, I think, we should have less discontent and less unrest in India than we have at present,—the Englishman receives only a small fine. Lately there was a case of resisting the police. The labourers of a man, under his orders, he being present, resisted the police in pulling down a fence. Master and labourers were brought up before the magistrate. The master was fined, and the labourers were sent to gaol for doing what their master had told them to do—they were Indians. Assaults upon Indians are punished with light fines, that are paid with a laugh or a sneer. A blow that kills, which is only too frequent in India, is treated in this way. A man lately had to pay a small fine of 25 rupees because he "only struck one blow and did not mean to kill." Presumably not, but he did kill, and the sum of 25 rupees (about £1, 13s.) is not a very big price for kicking your servant and killing him. He had "an enlarged spleen"—a reason for not striking, not a reason for a small fine.

These things are happening constantly in India. It is not as though they were rare. They are not. Men of all ranks in India are thus insulted. I have known a nobleman flogged with a riding-whip because he did not take off his hat to an Englishman he did not know—a well-known Sikh, who happened to be a very small man and, proud as he was, was not able to strike back again.

These things are all remembered; they pass from mouth to mouth, and all make an increasing bitterness. Those are points also that you want to understand when you are dealing with what is called Indian unrest and disaffection.[1]

[1] I had not time to deal with the retrial of acquitted persons—a monstrosity. During the years 1901–10 there were 284 of these, and in 25 cases the men concerned were hanged.

Then take the disadvantage that Indians have in education—popular, not university at all. Mr Gokhale brought in a Bill for universal education, which was thrown out, as the cost was too much. That is largely true; but Japan has been educating her people, and in forty years, beginning with gross illiteracy, Japan has so educated her boys and girls that the standard of literacy there is now higher than it is in America—one of the best educated countries in the world. Can you wonder that, talking over that one day, an Indian gentleman said to me: "We should be able to do the same if we had no alien government"? England would do well to attend to that matter, and remember that people are beginning to compare the results of English government in India and Japanese government in Japan.

Take another question—representation on the Indian Council, one of the messages brought over by the Congress delegates this year. What have they asked for? They have asked for three men to be elected by the Legislatures on the India Council out of nine. And in the Bill brought in two are suggested, not elected, as was asked for, but to be selected from a panel elected by the non-official members. Now, remember that "non-official members" includes men who are appointed by the Government; they are not all elected. That is where people juggle with words. Non-official people who are not elected are more servile to the Government than their own officials; and if you make up a panel of forty non-official members, and on that put a number of these appointees of the Government, and then ask the Secretary of State to choose, don't you think he will choose his own appointed people and make the whole election a farce and not a reality? It is no use to try that sort of trick with one of the cleverest peoples in the world. They see through a pretended liberty, and only despise the people who give it. One's only hope is that when the Bill comes to the Commons the Lords will have already amended it, and made it a real gift to India of some representation on her own Council by her own men, sent there by her own people.

And now we come to what is perhaps one

of the bitterest points of all—the Colonies. For the first time the population of India is being moved on this question, the question of the right to emigrate. Now you know the way it has grown up. English people come and take the country which really belonged to coloured people, and they are not able to carry on labour there because the climate does not suit them well; they ask for indentured coloured labour—and indenture is only slavery. There is no people like the English for being deceived by a word. If you tell lies, you call it "diplomacy," and then it is all right. You steal another man's lands, and you call it "annexation," and it is perfectly beneficent; and if you make men slaves, when you call it "indentured labour" you think it quite satisfactory. Indenture ought to be abolished in every country, for it is slavery of a very terrible kind. America has abolished it; why cannot you?

Now in South Africa the English people could not cultivate the soil, so they got indentured Indians to do it for them; and as long as the indenture lasted they were quite willing to take the labour, because it enabled them to lead very comfortable lives. England partly went to war in South Africa because of the bad treatment of the African-born people and of the Indians. And then she gave self-government to the people that she had conquered, and lets the state of the coloured people be worse than it ever was before. Now when the indenture had come to an end in South Africa, they said: How can we get rid of these people?—because they dare to trade. And the Indian is a clever trader, and he does not drink, and he lives much more simply, and the result was that he began to undersell the white man. That is where the difficulty comes in. So they said: We will put a tax on them, unless they will re-indenture themselves. That was the beginning of the £3 tax. A great many of these men only earn £12 a year altogether, and if a man pays £3 tax for himself, and £3 for his wife, there is not very much left out of the £12 a year to live upon. And so they said they would not pay. You can hardly blame them for it. Then they had to go away. Now some of those men had built up little businesses, had children born in the country. They have had forced sales; all their little earnings have gone, and they are sent back, poor again, to India. So things went on and on—you know the story very well, and it is changed now. But why the change? Because of the agitation in India. Because when Mr Gokhale called upon the Indian people they answered to his call. He asked for money, and they poured out more than he asked for. He asked for meetings, and they held meetings all over the country. The women came out and held meetings, a thing they have never done before, for, in this, Indian marriage was struck at, and the wife was turned into a mistress, and that roused the Indian women, and they came out to speak, and to give, and to agitate. And so dangerous did that become, so strong the feeling, so universal the protest, that the Viceroy, like a statesman, put himself at the head of the agitation and so prevented it from becoming a riot. Oh, I know some of you blamed him over here; but you were not in India to see the bitterness that had been aroused; and he saved India then from rioting by putting himself at the head of that agitation.

But India has learned her lesson from that. She has gained most of that which she asked for, and she has learned for the first time that when she speaks in public meetings for the sake of her exiled children, others will have to listen to her; and she will never forget her lesson, which has welded all the classes together and has made a nation feel its strength for the first time.

But it is not only in South Africa: Australia, New Zealand, Columbia, Vancouver—everywhere the same question is arising. Now take Australia. You may state the difficulty, if you like. It is a fair difficulty which is being put by the colonists, who say: Indians can live where we starve; Indians will take lower wages than we can live upon; we cannot come down to live as they live, therefore we won't let them into the country. It is an economic question upon which your colonists are feeling so strongly to-day, and it is fair to recognise that, for it is a question very difficult for the Labour men in this country to face. And remember, the Labour vote is all-powerful in a country like Australia—very much to the detriment of the country, if my Labour friends will allow me to say so, for no one class should have all the power in that way. North Australia cannot be cultivated except by people born in the tropics, and Australia cannot manage the northern sugar plantations with white men's labour only. Moreover, do you think a white Australia is possible with Japan wanting to colonise? How can the thousands of miles of northern coast be defended by a few white men against the incursion of the Japanese? Has Asia no rights in any part of the world that even her ocean must be white man's territory?

But it is not really only a question of labour. There was a Colonel Dantra, an M.D. in the Indian Medical Service, who wanted to go to Australia to set up a fruit farm, and he sent over to ask whether he could buy land, and he was told that as he was an Indian he could not go in. And how did they keep him out? By a law that unless an Indian can pass a language test he is not to be allowed to go in; and they may set the test in any language they like, modern Greek, Russian, Polish, Roumanian. The Indians are very clever in languages, but it is hopeless for them to try to pass such a test. That test was made at Mr Joseph Chamberlain's suggestion, for he said it would make them less angry than if you said plainly a coloured man must not come in. It seems to me more hateful because of its hypocrisy. And so the learned doctor, who certainly would not have upset the labour market, was told he could not go in and take up a fruit farm or other farm there. And so he remains discontented, and the whole thing spreads. Now what do you really propose to do with these complaints? You shut Indians out from the higher posts in their own country and only open the door to those over here of which I spoke. Not only in the Indian Civil Service, but in the Indian Medical Service, the Educational Service, the Engineering Service, all the highest posts are monopolised either by white men or by Indians who come over here. And when they come over they are not welcome. When they come over they find the two great Universities shut the doors upon them. Two Indians a year may be admitted in any Oxford college!—not must be, but may be. But there are hundreds of them who want to come. What right have you to say they shall not serve in their own country unless they are educated here, and then to make their lives a misery to them when they come by your contempt? That is the question you have to face. You go to these people, who are as highly civilised as yourselves, as highly educated in the educated classes as yourselves, man for man every whit as good as you are, and you say: We are going to monopolise all the best places; all the best posts are ours, all the most highly paid, and we will open a little crack of a door by which one or two of you may creep in if you come over to England to get educated and try very hard; but we will make things so disagreeable for you when you come that you will wish you had not come and will want to go back. I ask how far these things are to go? How long do you think you can claim the right to rule India when you shut her children out of her own government, and shut them now out of every other country as well over which your Union Jack is flying? Lord Meath came down to Madras a little while ago and addressed the students, and he praised the Union Jack and told them how proud they ought to be of it. Afterwards the students called on me to speak, and I said: "My Lord Meath, when you get back to the House of Lords, if you will ask members to make the Union Jack the protection of every Indian who is under it, then they will be proud of it; but so long as it cannot protect the Indian in the Colonies, don't think the Indian in India is going to be very, very proud of it floating above his head." I don't know whether Lord Meath will do anything of that sort; I don't much suppose he will. But the question has to be solved. Suppose the Colonies say: "We will not let them in," you cannot make them. The Empire in that is only a name. You know you cannot force on your self-governing Colonies an unrestricted immigration from any nation, Indian or anybody else. They have the right to rule in their own house, and—to reap the results of their ruling. The result will very likely be a Japanese invasion of Australia; but that is their business. If Australia were wise, she would welcome Indians to strengthen the Empire. I am not sure that I want them to do it, and I will tell you why. If they go on with their policy of shutting Indians out of every white man's country, the result will be that coloured men will begin to shut the white men out of the coloured countries. You went to war with China to force your right to go into China, and you said they were barbarians because they shut the door, and there ought to be an open door for white men. I agree; but there ought to be an open door for the coloured man as well. And they may think it worth while, if they are shut out from other countries, to shut out the white men. I believe it will lead more quickly to self-government in India, and that is why I am not sorry this policy should go on for a time. You cannot deny self-government if you do not cease shutting them out of other countries; India must be able to defend herself, if you cannot defend her. If that is what you want, you will get it. There must be some place for the coloured man in this world. A white skin is not everything. Where is the divine right of the white skin to go into other men's countries and to say that the coloured man shall not enter into the white country? It is a disgrace to raise this question of the colour of skin as a barrier among the citizens of this so-called British Empire. You cannot do it for long. India is beginning to understand her own strength; she is beginning to realise that you cannot always keep her as a slave; for to tie a man to the soil on which he was born is to make him a serf, as he was in the Middle Ages, when no man might go outside his own parish lest he should become a rogue and a vagabond. You would make the nation dishonoured that was civilised and mighty when your ancestors were wandering naked about your forests. These Indians that you scoff at and deride—they are civilised with a civilisation that goes back for thousands upon thousands and thousands of years. When they were free, they made the greatest literature that the world has ever known; and it is with the revival of the spirit of nationality that their intellectual greatness will once more show itself in works of originality and of power. With the loss of freedom they have gone down in their intellectual work; with the regaining of freedom they will rise to the mighty point that they occupied before. Even now they show their ability, and they are pleading with you for freedom. They are not demanding it roughly, as I am demanding it here; for I, a white, am speaking to you white men and women, and have the right to make you understand what you are doing to these our coloured friends on the other side of the world. They do not speak as brutally as I am speaking to you, but they feel. Oh, they would love you if you would let them; they ask you to give them their freedom, to let them be free men in a free country. Your Crown will be more secure. They know that England and India together are far stronger than England and India can ever be separately, and the possibility of an Empire for Great Britain rests on the co-operation of India.

And so I plead with you, who are English men and women. England was the mother of freedom, and these little islands of yours have grown into the centre of a world-wide Empire because of your love of liberty, your declaration that no slave could live on English soil, for wherever your flag floated there freedom was found beneath it. You, who gave shelter to Mazzini when all the tyrants in Europe would have seized him; you, who crowded your London streets to welcome Garibaldi, who freed Italy from the tyrants that oppressed her: you, who have been the sanctuary of the oppressed of every people—why, you gave shelter to Stepniak the Terrorist from Russia; you gave shelter to Kropotkin, the exile and the rebel. And now you, in your own country, deny the right of other men to seek for freedom, when you have welcomed every exile for freedom, and have spread over them your protecting sword and shield. No political exile was ever given up by England; no political crime was held by her to be reason to give a man over to gaol or to the scaffold. And yet the gaol and the scaffold are the means you are using to break down political freedom in India, and I plead with you to live up to your own old traditions, to be faithful to the memory of your past. Liberty is your birthright; oh, share your birthright with your Indian friends. Then India will become the buttress of your Empire. Her three hundred millions will be at your back whenever you are in difficulty with other countries. But the price of their loyalty is the gift of freedom; and until they are free you can never expect them to be loyal.